Praise
God of the

"Wide-ranging and accessible, *God of the Big Bang* builds a welcome bridge from evangelical Christianity to science. At a time when so many evangelicals feel threatened by science, Professor Wickman shows that contemporary science is not the enemy of faith."

Karl Giberson
Former President of the BioLogos Foundation, Author, Science & Religion Scholar-in-Residence at Stonehill College

"*God of the Big Bang* is a powerful statement by someone who has had a career in one of the most exciting areas of science and who asserts with energy and confidence that there is no conflict between science and her faith. Leslie Wickman's blending of personal experience and academic argument makes for an engaging read."

Nigel Cameron
Writer, Speaker, Bioethicist

"Pope John Paul II famously said that 'faith and reason are like two wings on which the human spirit ascends to contemplation of truth.' Yet many believe that faith and reason—and particularly faith and *science*—are in tension, even conflict. Are they right? Or is the alleged conflict a mere illusion? Leslie Wickman—an astronomy professor, a Christian believer, and a gifted thinker and writer—powerfully makes the case that it is an illusion that is 'perpetuated by fundamentalists' on both sides who operate from ignorance of what science actually shows, and who refuse to apply to the topic the critical thinking it deserves. *God of the Big Bang* is a valuable and timely contribution to public understanding of science and religion and the relationship between the two."

Robert P. George
McCormick Professor of Jurisprudence,
Princeton University

"If the science and faith debate has always seemed like a confusing shouting match between scientists, this is the book for you. Dr. Leslie Wickman brings her considerable scientific expertise and her faithful Christian commitment together to explain in a simple and clear way what science is and what sort of questions it can answer. There are no confusing debates or name-calling here, just an example of how a scientific mind helps us think about our faith."

Bethany Sollereder
Research Coordinator, University of Oxford

"Writing from her life's passion to break down the widely perceived wall between science and faith, astro-scientist Leslie Wickman clearly shows that one does not have to abandon one to embrace the other. 'A person can choose to be both a good scientist as well as a faithful Christian,' she writes in *God of the Big Bang*, embracing creation and the Bible as two great 'books' of God's revelation. With a humble, loving, and caring reading of both books, Professor Wickman contends in this fine work that science can even be an act of worship. And with this she encourages scientists and aspiring scientists to understand we need not choose between science and faith, but embrace both to the glory of God."

Calvin B. DeWitt

Professor of Environmental Science,
University of Wisconsin,
and Author of Song of a Scientist

Leslie A. Wic

GOD OF THE BIG BANG

HOW MODERN SCIENCE AFFIRMS THE CREATOR

LESLIE WICKMAN, Ph.D

Corporate Test Astronaut, Rocket Scientist, and Hubble Space Telescope Engineer

WORTHY®
PUBLISHING

Library of Congress Control Number: 2015930477

Creation is the primary and most perfect revelation of the Divine.

Thomas Aquinas (1224–1274)

Contents

Acknowledgments ....*xi*

Introduction ....*xv*

1 Family Star Parties:
A Plan and a Purpose 1

2 Is God Real? Evidence
for His Existence 13

3 Approach with Caution:
Using the Scientific Method 23

4 A Reasonable Faith:
Using Logic and Sound Arguments 39

5 The Bible: Its Evidence,
Interpretation, and Message................. 57

6 Genesis and Origins:
A Spectrum of Views............. 69

7 The Goldilocks Principle:
Just-Right for Life 85

8 Environmental Stewardship:
This Is My Father's World................... 113

9 The Universe:
Are We Alone? 145

Conclusion..*169*

Notes *173*

Acknowledgments

To my friends, advocates, and loved ones who have stood by me and supported me through the process of researching, writing, editing, and rewriting: thanks for believing in me and encouraging me!

My path to this book has been a long one, with many inspirations along the way, some divine and some human. My father, Walt Wickman, was the first to ignite my love of nature in general, and particularly my passion for astronomy, for which I am eternally grateful. My junior high biology teacher, Bill Riedel, challenged me to think more deeply about the origin and development of life. Solar astronomer Ron Cottrell's book *The Remarkable Spaceship Earth* was the first book I ever read that inspired me to look for the connections between nature and God's providence. Ron has since become a good friend and mentor to me, and his ongoing inspiration in my life is apparent in chapter 7.

My role at Azusa Pacific University (APU) in organizing our ongoing Science, Faith, and Culture (SFC) lecture series has afforded me the privilege of sitting at the feet of many great scholars from around the world as they share their thoughts on integrating their particular disciplines with the Christian faith. Talbot Seminary philosopher-theologian William Lane Craig's presentations on rational thought and clear logic were foundational for me, as reflected in chapter 4. Attorney and friend Jim Eriksen also helped to shape my thoughts on logic and reason in chapter 4.

Astrophysicists Hugh Ross and Jeff Zweerink, philosopher Kenneth Samples, and biochemist Fazale Rana—my friends at Reasons to Believe—have given numerous APU SFC lectures and written a plethora of books that have helped form my perspectives on science and faith, particularly with respect to the Goldilocks Principle (chapter 7), and extraterrestrial (ET) phenomena (chapter 9).

My astronomer friend Mark Ritter was also instrumental in helping me flesh out the attributes of the Goldilocks Principle (chapter 7). Chapter 5's section entitled "So Who Is Jesus?" was also heavily influenced by Mark's research.

Another frequent participant in APU's SFC series whom I must thank abundantly is science and religion scholar Denis Lamoureux, who generously shared his perspectives with me in the chapter 6 discussion of Genesis and origins.

Francis Collins, Ted Davis, Darrel Falk, and Deborah Haarsma of BioLogos have also increased my understanding of biological processes through their lectures and writings.

Calvin DeWitt has been my strongest mentor in the area of environmental stewardship and creation care, and I am forever grateful for his impact on my life and thinking. Much of his inspiration resonates in chapter 8.

I appreciate APU theology professors Marsha Fowler, Steve Wilkens, and Bill Yarchin for modeling scholarly writing about spiritual matters and for challenging me to read and understand Scripture in a scholarly way.

I'm also thankful to my theologian friends Bethany Sollereder and Josh Rasmussen for critiquing early versions of this book—their feedback greatly improved the content. Ultimately, thanks be to God for revealing himself in his creation!

Let them praise the name of the Lord,
For He commanded and they were created.

Psalm 148:5 (NASB)

Introduction

Starry, Starry Night

As AN ASTRONOMY professor, I often take groups of students outside on clear nights to look at the thousands of stars visible to the naked eye. Gazing at the heavens, people of all ages inevitably begin asking the same questions that have been asked since humans first inhabited this planet:

- Where did all this come from?
- How big is the cosmos?
- What's it all made of?
- How long has it been here?
- Was there anything before all this?

- Where are we going?
- How will it all end?
- Is there anyone else out there?

These questions are not just for scientists, but for all of us. Vincent van Gogh wrote his brother, Theo, saying, "The sight of stars always sets me dreaming."

Mark Twain's Huckleberry Finn said, "We had the sky up there, all speckled with stars, and we used to lay on our backs and look up at them, and discuss about whether they was made, or only just happened."

And King David wrote in the Bible's book of Psalms, "The heavens declare the glory of God; the skies proclaim the work of his hands. Day after day they pour forth speech; night after night they display knowledge" (Psalm 19:1–2).

Starry nights do that to people—they make us think and feel and wonder about the big questions in life. This is an essential part of the human condition, and we should never stop wondering about the mysteries of our world. In the spirit of free inquiry, no questions should ever be considered off-limits. None of us can claim to be so close to God that we have everything perfectly figured out. (Be very suspicious of anyone who suggests otherwise.)

Ultimately, on an individual level, all these ponderings are wrapped up in the very personal yet profound question of, "What am I doing here?" or perhaps, "What's the reason for my existence?"

As you're reading this, maybe you feel far from God, or perhaps you've done something you think he could never forgive you for, or maybe you're angry with God for something that's happened in your life. Maybe you feel that God is not good and loving or perhaps you wonder if faith in God really makes sense. Or maybe (as it was in my case) you're already a person of faith, but your beliefs need to be reconciled with your intellect and life experiences to strengthen your faith and permit you to share it more clearly.

Most of us search for meaning in our lives. We want to somehow make sense of everything. That's what having a spirit or spiritual dimension within ourselves is all about. People want to know that their lives mean something; that they have a purpose; that they can make a difference.

This book raises some thought-provoking questions that you may have been wrestling with or that will capture your imagination if you haven't. Regardless, as you read you'll start seeing these questions from a fresh perspective, one that shows you the Creator. In addition, each chapter was designed to spur ongoing conversations with other inquisitive minds among your friends, acquaintances, and even the strangers you encounter in everyday life.

I wrote this book for anyone who has ever wondered, like I did, how to reconcile what science and faith have to say about life's biggest questions. It's also for those skeptical of faith who fully believe that science is the only way to know anything and for faithful believers who distrust science and suspect its "motives." And it's for all those in between these two extremes who may be confused or put off by all the combative and nonproductive dialogue on the topic.

My hope is that by offering thoughtful consideration of these two separate but connected ways of knowing, this book will promote the kind of constructive dialogue that tears down the imaginary wall between science and faith. And in the process, you'll recognize more of the God who is big enough to encompass them both.

1 Family Star Parties: A Plan and a Purpose

THROUGHOUT MY LIFE, it seems that God has been preparing me to write this book. My interest in science began developing while I was a child, when my father took my brothers and me outside on clear, starry nights—a somewhat rare occurrence in the Pacific Northwest where I grew up. Looking through his telescope at the moon, stars, and planets sparked my early passion for astronomy and all things space-related.

Being raised in a Christian home, from as far back as I can remember, I had an underlying belief in God as the Creator of everything. At the same time my father, an engineer, was quite analytical. He had a strong interest in math and science and encouraged that interest in my brothers and me. And, at least in that way, I wanted to be like my dad.

Studious and geeky, possibly to the point of bordering on Asperger syndrome, I was painfully shy as a kid—at least until my family's move from Washington to Oregon forced me to start coming out of my shell. Due to the suddenness of the move, my older brother and I were temporarily sent to live with another family. That experience initiated years of hard, intentional work on my social skills.

The Great Divide

Whenever my brothers and I looked at the heavens, we understood that God was their Creator. My parents and the church taught us that the world was God's creation. But at school my science teacher taught something quite different. From his perspective, the facts of nature had nothing to do with God or religion.

Back then, my heart believed that God was the Creator, yet my mind didn't know how to integrate that conviction with science. How could the purely naturalistic theories of origins being taught in school mesh with my understanding of God?

When I was in junior high school, I was so concerned about the discrepancy between what I was learning at church versus what was being taught in my biology class that I took it upon myself to go through the book of Genesis in the Bible counting generations and adding up the years between Adam and Jesus just to try to figure out how much time might have passed between the first human being and the first century. That exercise helped me start researching my questions on my own.

As time went on, I continued studying both science and biblical interpretation. Through my research, it became increasingly clear that rather than contradicting each other, science and theology complement one another and together flesh out a more coherent view of the world. Too little information had created the dilemma that made me feel like I was supposed to choose between them. Deeper and more complete understanding of each discipline started resolving my angst and enabling me to embrace both science and theology.

Several scientists from the seventeenth century (Bacon, Galileo, and Newton) are among those credited with stating that "God is the author of two books: the Book of Scripture and the Book of Nature." Even earlier, Saint Augustine warned

Christians that they must be able to understand the relationship between science and Scripture:

> Usually, even a non-Christian knows something about the earth, the heavens, and the other elements of this world, . . . and this knowledge he holds to as being certain from reason and experience. Now, it is a disgraceful and dangerous thing for an infidel to hear a Christian, presumably giving the meaning of Holy Scripture, talking nonsense on these topics; and we should take all means to prevent such an embarrassing situation, in which people show up vast ignorance in a Christian and laugh it to scorn. The shame is not so much that an ignorant individual is derided, but that people outside the household of faith think our sacred writers held such opinions, and, to the great loss of those for whose salvation we toil, the writers of our Scripture are criticized and rejected as unlearned men.[1]

The more I learned by studying nature, the more I began standing in awe of nature's Creator. The intricacies and synergies—or uncanny collaborations—of creation have continually inspired me to worship the One who put it all together.

Unfortunately, there is indeed an *illusion* of conflict between science and religion, but that seems to be perpetuated by the fundamentalists at the polar extremes of this dialogue, those so thoroughly entrenched in their own positions that they cannot step back and think critically about their own perspectives.

A primary motivation in the writing of this book has been to help break down that perceived wall between science and faith, so that people—especially young people—realize it's not an either/or choice. A person does not have to leave his faith to pursue science, nor does someone have to reject science to be true to her faith. I didn't.

Fast-Forward

Over the years my research, work, and life experience have validated the compatibility of science and faith issues to the point that I frequently discuss them with family, friends, and people I meet in the normal course of my day. Sometimes that individual is a university student. Sometimes in my travels a person hears my background and asks one of the "big" questions of life. And sometimes I instigate a discussion with someone who shows an interest in either science or faith.

Scientific discoveries continue to surprise me with their potential to open up new opportunities to share my beliefs. In March 2014, after the Antarctica-based BICEP2 experiment announced possible evidence for gravity waves in the cosmic microwave background radiation,[2] an editor at CNN's Belief Blog invited me to write an opinion editorial. This article, which CNN provocatively titled "Does the Big Bang breakthrough offer proof of God?"[3] went viral. With over half a million views in less than a week, it ranked in the top five of the world's most shared news stories on social media. In the wake of the publicity it generated, Worthy Publishing contacted me to write this book.

Coincidentally (that's said facetiously because I don't really believe in random coincidences), the week before the BICEP2 news broke, I met with an editor friend who had been encouraging me to write a book on science and faith for several years. She advised me that to produce a successful book I'd need a public platform, an audience, and a publisher, then BOOM—two weeks later I had all three.

The discovery I wrote about for CNN made people around the world want to know more. Though space considerations prevented the entire piece from being posted on the blog, I supplied my original here for a fuller explanation of the correlation between faith and science in the light of this news:

> The recent news headlines on the detection of evidence for gravitational waves in the cosmic microwave background radiation—ripples in the space-time fabric of the universe—rocked the world of science. Touted as evidence for inflation (the rapid, faster-than-the-speed-of-light, early expansion of our newborn universe), confirming the gravity waves predicted by Einstein's theory of general relativity, and lending credence to the idea of a grand unified theory; this is big news.
>
> But what are the implications of this new discovery for the Christian worldview? Insofar as it provides new evidence for the Big Bang, it provides strong support for the Judeo-Christian worldview. The prevalent theory of cosmic origins prior to the Big Bang theory was the Steady State theory, which stated that the universe had always existed and was therefore self-existent without a beginning that necessitated a cause. However, this new evidence

lends further support to the Big Bang theory, which tells us that our universe had a beginning.

If the universe had a beginning, by the simple logic of cause and effect, there must have been an agent—separate and apart from the effect—that caused it. Sounds a lot like Genesis 1:1 to me: "In the beginning God created the heavens and the earth."

All of us devout Christians are concerned about a faithful reading of Scripture, but a reading true to the biblical text requires hard work. It's not just about opening the Bible and reading whatever we find there from a twenty-first-century American perspective. The context must also be studied. In addition we need to evaluate the culture, the genre, the authorship, and the original audience as they flesh out the intended meaning. By combining these various aspects, we see that what is being communicated in the origins passages of Genesis 1 and 2 is a theological message rather than a scientific one.

The creation message tells us that God created a special place for humans to live and thrive and be in communion with him. It also communicates that God wants a relationship with each of us and makes provisions for us to have fellowship with him, even after we rebel against him.

Genesis was never intended to be a detailed scientific handbook describing how God created. If it were and the author foreshadowed references to the Big Bang, gravity waves, dark matter, and dark energy; the text would have been confusing at best, and at worst maybe even frightening. If concepts that we still struggle to understand today were written about thousands of years ago, the text of Genesis would have been completely incomprehensible to its original audience.

Most of the time, our view of God is not big enough. We tend to be more comfortable keeping him in a box where we can pretend to comprehend him. But an infinite God is not constrained by our limited, finite human understanding. When he doesn't act the way we think he should, we may feel like the children of Narnia in C. S. Lewis' beloved tale—*The Lion, the Witch and the Wardrobe*. While expressing their fear of Aslan (the Lion that represented Jesus), they were told: "'Course he isn't safe. But he's good."

The God who reveals himself through the biblical account of creation, as well as through scientific discoveries, may not fit our expectations, but he is good. A better understanding of each discipline informs our understanding of the other.

Science and faith are not in an "either/or" competition. The trick is in seeing how they fit together. A person can choose to be both a good scientist as well as a faithful Christian. If God is truly the Creator, then he will reveal himself through what he's created, and science is a tool that can be used to uncover those wonders. Properly practiced, science can be an act of worship in looking at God's revelation of himself in nature.

It seems that this cycle of new scientific discoveries, followed by an adjustment in our interpretation of Scripture relative to our understanding of God's interaction with the physical world, keeps repeating itself. A few examples include:

- Galileo's empirical evidence refuting the geocentric view of the cosmos
- Darwin's proposition of random mutations and natural selection for biological evolution
- Hubble, Gamow, Penzias, Wilson, and others' work showing evidence for a cosmic Big Bang beginning

Will Christians experience another crisis of faith if we discover convincing evidence for the multiverse hypothesis, or extraterrestrial intelligent life? Maybe so, but by breaking this cycle and taking God out of the box, we can worship the Creator as he really is—not safe, but good.

And, by discovering more reasons to believe in his existence, we'll learn even more about who he is.

2 Is God Real? Evidence for His Existence

DOES GOD EXIST? That's one of the most important of life's big questions. As soon as I start thinking about it, another basic question quickly arises in my analytical mind: "Can anyone ever really *prove* that God exists?"

Of course, Immanuel Kant and others would say that God's existence can never be proven. And truthfully, if we could fully prove God's existence, what room would be left for faith and free will? If God's existence were as empirically knowable as other physical realities (like the sun or the wind, for example), a person would have to be in terrible denial *not* to believe.

Still, perhaps the idea of proving God's existence depends on what we mean when using the word *proof*, which has different meanings within different contexts, especially in today's postmodern world. For example, a scientist might refer to "empirical proof," something that can be verified using one or more of the five physical senses. Or a forensic specialist might refer to "logical proof," as in cause and effect. An attorney might refer to "legal proof," as in "beyond a reasonable doubt" or "a preponderance of the evidence." Personally, in the discussion about proof of God, I prefer the following question: "What would constitute adequate evidence for you to concede the existence of God?"

Classical Arguments

As a scientist, empirical evidence and rational arguments are very appealing. There are a number of well-known and often-used arguments for God's existence, which have been called by various names over the ages. Their essentials are summarized in the following four argument strategies:

1. the cosmological argument
2. the ontological argument
3. the anthropological argument
4. the teleological argument

The first three of these categories are discussed in this chapter, and the fourth (the teleological argument) is addressed in chapter 7.

The Cosmological Argument

This argument in various forms has been credited to a variety of sources—from Plato and Aristotle to medieval Muslim and Jewish philosophers, as well as to Saint Thomas Aquinas. Many versions are inspired by the question, "Why is there something rather than nothing?"

Perhaps the simplest version, the Kalām cosmological argument, uses the logic of cause and effect, reasoning that anything that begins to exist has a cause. Thus, if the physical universe had a beginning (as both astrophysics and the book of Genesis tell us), something, or *Someone*, must have caused it.

This argument is pretty much the same as Aristotle's First Cause, or the Prime Mover concept: everything that happens is caused by something else, and everything (except the first thing) that causes something, is itself caused by something else. If you trace this line of reasoning back far enough (and avoid going crazy in the process), you eventually end up at the First Cause—the uncaused cause, the unmoved mover, or the Prime Mover. Aristotle thought this causal agent must itself be eternal, perfect, unchanging, and independent of anything else. Following this same line of reasoning, Saint Thomas Aquinas concluded that the "First Cause" must be God.

Modern-day theologian and philosopher William Lane Craig explained the cosmological argument by stating that since the universe began to exist (that is, it did not always exist), it is not a so-called necessary being and, therefore, it is not self-explanatory with respect to its existence. Since whatever begins to exist has a cause, there must be something that ultimately preceded it: an eternal, transcendent cause of the universe. Thus, the only noncontingent, self-explanatory "necessary being" is God.[1]

The Ontological Argument

Originated by Saint Anselm of Canterbury, this argument uses abstract reasoning. Adapted and modified by others such as René Descartes, Gottfried Leibniz, and Kurt Godel, it goes something like this: anyone who would even consider that God does exist is, in a sense, admitting that there is a God. That's because part of what is meant when speaking of

God is that he's a "perfect being," and a God who exists is more perfect than one who does not. If perfection is a part of the concept of God and if God's perfection implies his existence, then to speak of God as a perfect being is therefore to imply that he exists. Still with me?

Seventeenth-century French mathematician Blaise Pascal hinted at this concept with his notion of the "God-shaped vacuum" within every person. The fact that we have within us *the idea of God* suggests that God is its cause. Mankind's "God-consciousness" (or simply our thoughts of God) implies a God who imprinted such a consciousness on him.

This God-consciousness is universal in that it is experienced by humans everywhere, regardless of time, place, culture, and society. In more recent times, Christian philosopher Alvin Plantinga has updated the basic reasoning behind Anselm's argument by using the logic of necessity and possibility.

The Anthropological Argument

The third classical argument encompasses assertions from moral conscience and from religious experience. This argument is based on evidence for the human spirit. Our spiritual dimension differentiates us as human beings from animals, and it is evidenced by our quest for meaning and purpose in life.

When we worship, we are able to think abstractly and mentally experience the spiritual domain. We also think abstractly and are often inspired to reach beyond ourselves when we admire art, nature, music, or architecture. Reasoning by inference to the best explanation, these distinctly human spiritual traits are said to point to an intelligent, moral, and personal Creator.

The moral component to this argument asserts that the universal built-in human awareness of right and wrong, also referred to as "moral conscience" or "natural law," implies a moral Creator who put it there. Saint Paul the apostle writes in his letter to the Romans, "the requirements of the law are written on their hearts, their consciences also bearing witness, and their thoughts now accusing, now even defending them" (2:15). One paraphrase of the Bible reads, "God's law is not something alien, imposed on us from without, but woven into the very fabric of our creation. There is something deep within them that echoes God's yes and no, right and wrong" (MSG).

Former atheist turned theologian C. S. Lewis writes in his book *Mere Christianity* about the implied standards people appeal to when arguing with each other. The specific example he gives is of two men arguing over a seat. One isn't necessarily saying to the other that:

> his behavior does not happen to please him. He is appealing to some kind of standard of behavior which he expects the other man to know about. And the other man very seldom replies: "To hell with your standard!" . . . It looks, in fact, very much as if both parties had in mind some kind of Law, or Rule of fair play, or decent behavior, or morality, or whatever you like to call it, about which they really agreed . . . [Otherwise] they could not quarrel in the human sense of the word. Quarreling means trying to show that the other man is in the wrong. And there would be no sense in trying to do that unless you and he had some sort of agreement as to what Right and Wrong are.[2]

Our consciences display objective, absolute moral values as opposed to societal or personally advantageous ones. We humans are able to make difficult moral choices that lead us to perform honorable and courageous, self-sacrificing actions that are hard to explain from merely the self-preserving motivations of evolutionary natural selection.

The religious experience component to this argument claims that personal religious experiences affirm God's existence to those who have them. This component can be explained as follows: A person can only perceive that which exists, so God must exist because there are people who have experienced him. While religious experiences can only constitute direct evidence of God's existence for those privileged enough to have them, the fact that there are many people who claim to have had such experiences constitutes indirect evidence of God's existence, even to those who personally haven't had them.

Putting It All Together

In addition to the first three strategies, there is the teleological argument, also known as the fine-tuning argument or the argument from design, which will be covered in detail in chapter 7.

For now, let's circle back and summarize these arguments:

1. The cosmological argument says that effects have causes, and a beginning must have a Beginner.

2. The ontological argument says that the fact that we have in us the idea of God implies that God must be its cause.

3. The anthropological argument points out the existence of universal absolute moral values, as well as the assertion that God must exist because there are people who have experienced him.

4. As is described in chapter 7, the teleological argument argues from the standpoint of the amazing design, order, and complexity of the universe.

My hope and prayer is that this chapter has inspired your mind for science to rejoice with your heart for God. And that whenever you think of these evidences for the reality of God and see how everything in science and nature fits together, you'll break out in a Snoopy-dance of celebration!

Understanding how to use the scientific method adds even more joy to the victory dance of reconciling science with your faith.

3 Approach with Caution: Using the Scientific Method

A S A SCIENTIST, I frequently make observations and formulate hypothetical explanations. Then, with enough information, I make predictions, do experiments, and create models or theories to try to answer questions about nature. Contemporary scientists generally refer to this iterative process as the scientific method. The basic steps of this process flow as depicted in the following diagram.

OBSERVE -> HYPOTHESIZE -> PREDICT -> TEST ->
CHECK RESULTS ->MODIFY AS REQUIRED
-> REPEAT

Scientists use this approach to achieve an as yet unfalsified explanation to describe observed phenomena. That permits us to make accurate predictions that lead to a better comprehension of the physical universe. The scientific enterprise attempts to understand the wide variety of nature's effects as resulting from the action of a relatively small number of basic causes or forces, acting in a virtually unlimited variety of combinations.

To put it another way, scientists use the scientific method to try to simplify our understanding of the world and the way things work. The big, revolutionary idea behind the scientific method is that simple truths about nature are really the end goal of science rather than the unattainable starting point assumed by the early Greek natural philosophers who paved the way for modern science. Because of this, inductive reasoning is well-suited to achieve this purpose. The inductive process is more or less the deductive process in reverse: we start with many observations of, and experiments with, nature and move toward a few durable explanations of how things work.

No Proof!

It's important to keep in mind that the scientific method by its very nature is only capable of disproving, rather than proving theories. This induction-based approach is structured to investigate whether experimental results are consistent with hypotheses and theories. If the test results are not consistent, then the hypothesis or theory is disproven; if the test results are consistent, then additional support is accumulated for that particular hypothesis or theory.

Indeed, the scientific enterprise looks for the best explanation of natural phenomena currently possible given the existing evidence. Credible scientists realize that new evidence could be discovered at any time that would overturn the best theories of today. Francis Bacon, often thought of as the "father of modern science," fully understood these implications. He said: "Our method, though difficult in its operation, is easily explained. It consists in determining the degrees of certainty."[1]

A more contemporary quote from the late Nobel Prize–winning physicist Richard Feynman echoes Bacon: "Scientific knowledge is a body of statements of varying degrees of certainty—some most unsure, some nearly sure, but none absolutely certain."[2]

Such statements apply equally to all scientific endeavors, but Bacon's words seem almost prophetic when we consider the discoveries of quantum physics more than three hundred years after they were published. Commenting on the newly emerging theory and reflecting the deterministic outlook of modernity (often identified with belief in God), Albert Einstein wrote in a 1926 letter to Max Born: "I, at any rate, am convinced that *He* [God] does not throw dice."[3]

Science author and geologist Steven Schafersman writes this about the scientific method:

> The scientific method has proven to be the most reliable and successful method of thinking in human history . . . [C]ritical thinking is perhaps the most important skill a student can learn in school . . . since if you master its skills, you know how to think successfully and reach reliable conclusions, and such ability will prove valuable in any human endeavor . . . Since critical thinking and scientific thinking are . . . the same thing, only applied for different purposes, it is therefore reasonable to believe that if one learns scientific thinking . . . one learns, at the same time, the most important skill a student can possess—critical thinking. This, to my mind, is perhaps the foremost reason for college students to study science, no matter what one's eventual major, interest, or profession.[4]

So we see broad acceptance of the premise that the scientific method can help us as we seek truth. But is Schafersman right? Can this approach help us pursue truth in areas other than the natural sciences? Are some subjects beyond the scope of scientific investigation?

Some contend that science and faith are mutually exclusive realms because spiritual matters cannot be detected or tested by natural, empirical means. But others disagree. When it comes to matters of science and theology, the search for understanding typically manifests itself in different ways. Science is concerned with discovering and understanding natural phenomena; the domain of science is the natural world. This methodology seeks to know how things are, not so much why they are that way, nor how they should be.

On the other hand, theology is concerned with the source, purpose, and meaning of everything; the domain of theology is nature's purpose.

Better Together

Science and theology each have their place and should serve to complement rather than contradict each other. The study of nature through science and the pursuit of God through

27

faith are both ways of seeking the truth about reality. Just as with faith and science, there are dual explanations for almost every question in life. If one explanation addresses ultimate causes, another might address mechanistic processes. For example, I might ask the question, "Why was I born?" My parents might answer, "Because we wanted another child." Yet a doctor's response might address the biological processes of sperm and ovum uniting and producing a baby. They aren't mutually exclusive, and both can be right, leading to a fuller understanding of the whole.

As mentioned in chapter 1, a lack of understanding about either science or theology can make people think they must choose one or the other. But a deeper and more complete understanding of each enables us to embrace them both without contradiction. If we start with the simple notion that truth exists about both God and nature, then those absolute truths cannot logically contradict each other. Any appearance of conflict must therefore stem from incomplete knowledge or flawed interpretation of the evidence. The more we correctly understand about each subject, the better understanding we have of the whole. Our studies of both God and nature should inform and enlighten each other, contributing to a clearer and more complete picture of ultimate truth.

Our progress both as individuals and as a society to truth about God and truth about nature are iterative: we might take two steps forward in our understanding, followed by a corrective step backward as we continue our explorations. This is consistent with the scientific method, which, when properly practiced, holds knowledge tentatively, realizing that new evidence might be discovered at any time that would make previous scientific theories invalid, and require new iterations in our interpretation of the physical world.

Improving upon Ideas

During the Renaissance, the scientific method was used to test the Aristotelian view of the sun moving around the earth. Copernicus proposed and later Galileo made telescopic observations providing evidence showing that the earth revolves around the sun, not the other way around. The former idea had been asserted as an obvious truth until newly acquired empirical evidence made this scientific correction possible. As it often does, the scientific process allowed humankind to view traditionally held notions from a broader frame of reference.

A similar paradigm shift or thought revolution occurred in advancing from Newtonian physics to relativity theory and quantum mechanics.

Without delving into the specific details, suffice it to say that humankind's comprehension of scientific concepts like gravity, time, and space itself (which scientists and laypeople alike thought were fairly well understood) was dramatically altered in the process.

In much the same way, no mere human can seriously claim to have God or Christianity completely figured out. Jesus' life and teachings presented a paradigm shift to the theology of his time and culture, and we still struggle today to understand and apply the full implications of that shift. Our scientific understanding is always evolving as we discover more about the natural world—just as my faith is always evolving as I lean in, trust, and discover more of God.

As 1 Corinthians 13:12 says, "For now we see through a glass, darkly; but then face to face: now I know in part; but then shall I know even as also I am known" (KJV). While the apostle Paul's words were intended to apply to our knowledge and understanding of God, they also serve as a useful metaphor for our knowledge and understanding of his creation. This verse points out that our access to truth is moderated in this life by partial knowledge, limited understanding, and imperfect interpretation of the data. That's a good reason for us to practice our disciplines with healthy amounts of modesty, humility, and even skepticism.

Charles Darwin held an opinion relevant to this discussion: "In scientific investigation, it is permitted to invent any hypotheses and if it explains various large and independent classes of facts, it rises to the ranks of well-grounded theory."[5] Consider also the following two statements—one from 2003, the other from the third century:

> JEFFREY NICHOLS, TWENTY-FIRST CENTURY: Science concerns itself with ideas about the world that can be tested, at least in principle. To be tested here means to be put into practice and seen to work . . . So can there be a science of spirit? I believe there can. We simply need to devise testable hypotheses about the nature of spirit . . . Spirit, because of its high complexity, has the ability to control matter. If we find complex and measurable material structures behaving in ways that cannot be explained by the properties of matter, we may postulate that spirit is at work. [6]

Minucius Felix, third century:

If upon entering some home you saw that everything there was well-tended, neat, and decorative, you would believe that some master was in charge of it, and that he himself was superior to those good things. So too in the home of this world, when you see providence, order, and law in the heavens and on earth, believe there is a Lord and Author of the universe, more beautiful than the stars themselves and the various parts of the whole world.[7]

In other words, as we make observations of nature, if we perceive order and complexity that exceed the normal operation of the laws of nature as we know them, then we can hypothesize that there is something extraordinary or supernatural at work. So perhaps the scientific method can be used as a tool to organize our thought processes and help us pursue greater understanding in matters of spirit as we seek out truth in various disciplines.

At the very least, the scientific method can be seen as a tool for discovering God's creativity and wisdom in the wonders of nature.

Great Minds

From the outset of the scientific enterprise through the present day, many prominent scientists have believed that science was a means for discovering truth in the physical, created world. Francis Bacon confirmed this perspective by quoting King Solomon's words in Proverbs 25:2, "It is the glory of God to conceal a thing, but the glory of a king to search it out."[8]

He was also one of several devoted Christ-followers instrumental in the development of the modern scientific method:

- Roger Bacon, Franciscan friar (1214–1294; an early advocate of the scientific method)
- Francis Bacon, professing Christian (1561–1626; England's "father of modern science")
- Galileo Galilei, devout Catholic (1564–1642; provided observational evidence for the heliocentric—sun-centered—model of our solar system)
- Robert Hooke, son of a minister/curate (1635–1703; made significant scientific contributions in cell biology, astrophysics, telecommunications, and transportation)

- Isaac Newton, student of theology (1642–1727; made significant scientific contributions in mechanics, gravity, optics, and calculus)

Let's also remember Nicolaus Copernicus, the Polish monk who in 1530 made a strong case for reviving the ancient (but unaccepted) Greek heliocentric model of the solar system originally proposed by Aristarchus. And Johannes Kepler, a German Protestant persecuted for his faith. In about 1619, he came up with his three laws of planetary motion, making sense of the heliocentric model through the realization that the planetary orbits were elliptical rather than circular. Without these two giants of early astronomical science, Galileo might have kept his telescopic observations of sunspots, craters on the moon, Venus' phases, and Jupiter's moons to himself and never have had his famous battle with the Church.

Furthermore, Christian apologist Michael Covington makes these points about the harmony between faith and science:

1. Modern science arose in Christianized Western Europe.

2. Jews, Christians, and Muslims believe in a Creator who made an orderly, rational, understandable universe and gave us permission to investigate and utilize it, thereby legitimizing science and technology.

3. Conversely, Animists believe that rocks, trees, etc. (things we think of as inanimate objects) have souls, and that we should not tamper with nature for fear of offending the spirits.

4. Most Hindus and Buddhists generally believe that the physical world is an illusion or distraction that we should try to transcend or get free of.

5. Atheists cannot even explain why it is possible for us to understand the universe.[9]

As Francis Bacon and others have argued, humans are not very good at understanding God's creation intuitively.

The demise of Aristotle's First Principles (which included the "obvious" notions that the earth was at the center of everything, that everything else moved in perfect circles around it, and that the celestial objects were perfect while the earth was imperfect) affirm this reality. It's also echoed in various passages of Scripture. Isaiah 55:9 says, "For as the heavens are higher than the earth, so are my ways higher than your ways and my thoughts than your thoughts" (NRSV). And, to revisit 1 Corinthians 13:12 (MSG): "We don't yet see things clearly. We're squinting in a fog, peering through a mist. But it won't be long before the weather clears and the sun shines bright! We'll see it all then, see it all as clearly as God sees us, knowing him directly just as he knows us!"

The Judeo-Christian tradition promotes belief in a God who created an orderly, rational, knowable cosmos, and invites his creatures to investigate his creation. Using the scientific method reveals knowledge not only of nature, but also of the Creator. (Other passages of Scripture attest to this theme—Psalm 19:1–2, 34:8; 97:6; Romans 1:19–20; 1 Thessalonians 5:21.)

While I was working on NASA's Hubble Space Telescope Program, whenever something came up to delay our launch date, my colleagues joked that just as God destroyed the legendary Tower of Babel, he didn't want us humans to accomplish too much too soon, or in this case, see too far or too much just yet. (It's been estimated that the Hubble Telescope expanded the amount of visible space by a factor of 700!) I think that little joke reflects our innate understanding of the apostle Paul's statement in Romans 1:20: "For since the creation of the world God's invisible qualities—his eternal power and divine nature—have been clearly seen, being understood from what has been made."

Our recent discoveries with the Hubble Telescope and other astronomical observatories have unveiled a universe even more extravagantly beautiful, intricately collaborative, orderly, and awe inspiring than we ever imagined. This points us to an orderly and consistent Creator who cares extravagantly for his creation and who wants us to find him through his creation. The scientific method helps us do that.

So do logic and reason.

4 A Reasonable Faith: Using Logic and Sound Arguments

IS THERE EVIDENCE that actually supports the Christian faith? Is Christianity true?

Taking a closer look at both faith and reason has helped me answer that question. The Greek word for faith is *pistis*—it means confidence, commitment, conviction, or trust. This word conveys the idea of persevering in the beliefs that someone has embraced. People persist in their faith because they are convinced it's true. That's why I live life the way I do.

Logic's Laws

Regardless of whether someone is an analytical person like me, the distinction between whether something is "true" or "false" only has meaning if sound reason applies. Without logic there could be no such thing as true or false. The notion of logic includes right reason and valid inferences. Reason requires systematic consistency, including adherence to the laws of logic and correspondence with the relevant facts. Basic logic can be grasped by understanding its fundamental laws of Identity, Non-contradiction, Excluded Middle, and Rational Inference:

- The Law of Identity says that something is true if and only if it is true;
- The Law of Non-contradiction says that contradictory statements cannot simultaneously be true;
- The Law of the Excluded Middle says that one of two mutually contradictory statements has to be true; there is no third, or "undecided" option; and
- The Law of Rational Inference says that if A = B, and B = C, then A must = C.

For example, if I say, "My foot is twelve inches long," then that statement is true if and only if my foot measures one foot in length. And it can't simultaneously be true that my foot is not twelve inches long (even though that might have been true when I was younger). Further, it must be true that my foot is either twelve inches long or it is not—there is no undecided middle option. And by rational inference, if the length of my foot is equal to the length of someone else's foot that is twelve inches long, then my foot must also be twelve inches long. (I do, by the way, have unusually large feet for a woman.)

It would be nearly impossible to get along in the real world without logic. Even the thought process involved in preparing to cross a busy street would be a challenge: Is there a car coming or not? Maybe that object that looks like a car is simultaneously moving and not moving, or maybe it's simultaneously something else altogether.

So logic is pretty much synonymous with right reason. It is necessary in everyday life and in many fields of study. The study of religion is no different.

Catholic theologian Raimon Panikkar applies this thought process to a person's faith:

> A believing member of a religion in one way
> or another considers his religion to be true.
> Now, the claim to truth has a certain built-in

exclusivity. If a given statement is true, its contradictory [statement] cannot also be true. And if a certain human tradition claims to offer a universal context for truth, anything contrary to that "universal truth" will have to be declared false.[1]

In this era of postmodernity, the notions of "true" and "false" (as well as "universal truth") have been widely questioned. In many circles they've been replaced by the concept of moral relativity. Many college students and young adults claim: "that may be true for you, but not for me." Nevertheless, if a rational person commits to something as "true," that requires a simultaneous acknowledgment that contradictory claims must logically be untrue, or false.

Throughout time human beings have recognized the importance of using logic to decide what is true and what is not and then basing their spiritual beliefs upon this right reason. B. B. Warfield wrote that "Faith is the gift of God; but it does not in the least follow that the faith God gives is irrational faith, that is, a faith without grounds in right reason."[2]

C. S. Lewis elaborated on this idea by saying that faith is not "the intention to believe what you want to believe in the face of evidence to the contrary," nor is it "the power of believing what we know to be untrue."[3]

Using Logic and Reason

The Bible itself demonstrates this use of reason and evidence to support the truth of Christ's identity as the Son of God—fully human, fully divine. Mark 2:10–11 records the way Jesus backed up his words with a miracle. Jesus said: "But that you may know that the Son of Man has power on earth to forgive sins," then he turned to the paralytic and said, "I say to you, arise, take up your bed, and go to your house" (NKJV). Then the paralytic did just that!

In John 15:24, Jesus said: "If I had not done among them the works which no one else did, they would have no sin; but now they have seen and also hated both Me and My Father" (NKJV).

Again in Luke 16:31, Jesus showed his frustration with stubborn human hearts and heads in the face of reason and evidence when he said: "If they do not listen to Moses and the Prophets, they will not be persuaded even if someone rises from the dead" (NASB). Then Jesus did just that!

Early Christian apostles also used reason to show that Jesus was the Messiah, the Christ. In Acts 17:2–3, we read:

Then Paul, as his custom was, went in to them, and for three Sabbaths reasoned with them from the Scriptures, explaining and demonstrating that the Christ had to suffer and rise again from the dead, and saying, "This Jesus whom I preach to you is the Christ" (NKJV).

Later, in Acts 18:28, we read: "for he [Apollos] vigorously refuted the Jews publicly, showing from the Scriptures that Jesus is the Christ" (NKJV). As Christ's followers today we, too, need to use reason and evidence to find out more about him in order to support and share our faith.

Using Astronomy, Physics, Anthropology, and More

Of the biggest contemporary challenges to the Christian faith, one goes something like this: "Since many philosophers claim that science has explained our origins, is the idea of God still necessary?" Sometimes this challenge may be phrased a little differently, but it all comes down to the same basic question: "Does Christianity really make sense in the light of logic, reason, and science?"

Questions like this haunted me throughout my public school education and on into college. Eventually I decided to investigate the actual evidence for myself. Growing up in the Christian tradition, I had accepted and followed what I'd been taught from a very young age as being true. Yet after being introduced to the practice of critical thinking during my college days, I went through a period of questioning and reevaluating what I'd learned and believed as a child.

In the marketplace of ultimate worldviews, I realized that the idea of a perfect God who created the universe and desired a freely chosen, loving relationship with us made the most sense. Sending his Son to restore our relationship with him made it possible for me to know him. That option rang true. Instead of simply accepting what others had taught me, a combination of my own life experiences coupled with a rational evaluation of the alternatives in light of the evidence resulted in my making a truth commitment of my own.

The more I continued to study, the more I saw how scientific findings in biology, physics, and astronomy all support belief in God. Nature's evidence is compelling.

The Big Bang

Some Christians cringe when they hear references to the Big Bang, but this scientific model of the origin of the universe is much more "God-friendly" than its predecessor. The earlier Steady State model reflects Carl Sagan's famous statement that "the universe is all that is, or was, or ever will be." In other words, the Steady State model says that the universe has always existed; therefore, there is no need to explain its beginning.

Conversely, as mentioned in the discussion of the cosmological argument (see chapter 2), the logic of cause and effect infers that every effect has a cause, so everything that begins to exist must have a cause. Because the Big Bang "effect" marks the beginning of space, time, matter, and energy, there must have been something—or Someone—that caused it. Sir Arthur Eddington, who experimentally confirmed Einstein's general theory of relativity, lamented this finding: "Philosophically, the notion of a beginning to the present order is repugnant to me and I should like to find a genuine loophole."[4]

Philosopher and atheist advocate Kai Nelson admits, "Suppose you suddenly hear a loud bang . . . and you ask me, 'What made that bang?' and I reply, 'Nothing, it just happened.' You would not accept that."[5]

Physicist Stephen Hawking claims, "Almost everyone now believes that the universe, and time itself, had a beginning at the Big Bang."[6]

Further, contrary to popular opinion, the Big Bang was not a chaotic explosion, but rather a very highly ordered event requiring vast amounts of information. Hawking wrote, "If the rate of expansion one second after the Big Bang had been smaller by even one part in a hundred thousand million million, the universe would have re-collapsed before it ever reached its present state."[7] However, if the expansion rate were any faster, matter would have spread out too rapidly to allow galaxies, stars, planets, or anything else (like you or me!) to form.

Another prominent astrophysicist, George Smoot, described the creation event as "finely orchestrated."[8] Mathematical physicist Roger Penrose, an associate of Hawking, showed that the highly ordered initial state of the universe is something that could not have just randomly occurred even by the slimmest chance.[9]

When acclaimed British astrophysicist Fred Hoyle calculated the miniscule probability that carbon atoms—necessary for life—would have precisely the required resonance for abundant production by nuclear fusion in stars, he said that his atheism was greatly shaken, adding his famous line, "A common sense interpretation of the facts suggests that a superintellect has monkeyed with physics."[10]

Princeton theoretical physicist Freeman Dyson echoes this impression: "In some sense, the universe knew we were coming." In other words, many highly regarded scientists recognize that the Big Bang creation event was much too finely tuned and improbable to be some cosmic accident.

Much more scientific evidence will be explored in chapter 7, but for now we'll move on to some of the other arguments for the reason and veracity of the Christian faith.

Moral Law, History, and Archaeology

The anthropological argument was touched on in chapter 2, but the morality piece of this argument also supports science. The idea of moral law asserts that the existence and universal nature of objective moral values—evidenced by human awareness of right and wrong, also referred to as "moral conscience" or "natural law"—implies a moral Creator (like the Judeo-Christian God described in the Bible) who put it there.

Next, the historical argument claims that history provides evidence for the truth of the Christian faith. Both history and archaeology corroborate the authenticity of biblical events, people, and prophecies. This evidence includes the fact that belief in God has permeated human history—transcending time, place, culture, and society. The history of the Christian Church can be traced all the way back to about 30 AD in Palestine. (Estimated dates for Jesus' birth range from about 7 BC to 1 AD.) The Christian day of worship became Sunday in about 30 AD, which was a dramatic shift from the Jewish Sabbath day of worship (Saturday).

In alliance with historical evidence, the archaeological argument points out that many biblical accounts as well as cultural practices and traditions in more than 25,000 sites have been corroborated through archaeology. It has confirmed specific biblical events that were previously doubted. Ancient dated coins have been found that depict the people and places mentioned in the Bible. Numerous sacred sites, relics, and ruins have been identified in and around Jerusalem.

Keith Schoville, professor emeritus of Hebrew and Semitic Studies at the University of Wisconsin-Madison, states, "It is important to realize that archaeological excavations have produced ample evidence to prove unequivocally that the Bible is not a pious forgery. Thus far, no historical statement in the Bible has proven false on the basis of evidence retrieved through archaeological research."[11]

Nelson Glueck, the late biblical archaeologist, rabbi, and former president of the Jewish Theological Seminary at Hebrew Union College and the Jewish Institute of Religion, wrote: "It may be stated categorically that no archaeological discovery has ever controverted a biblical reference."[12]

William Albright, the late archaeologist, biblical scholar, and linguist, wrote: "Discovery after discovery has established the accuracy of innumerable details [of the Bible]."[13] In my recent trip to Israel, I was fortunate enough to see some of this archaeological evidence firsthand, notably at such places as the Temple Mount in Jerusalem, the City of David, the Mount of Olives, the Garden of Gethsemane, the Sea of Galilee, Bethlehem, Nazareth, and the Qumran Caves.

Overall, the science of archaeology strongly confirms the context of the Bible. There are many examples of biblical references that were once thought to be unlikely, only to have archaeology later show that the people and places referred to did, in fact, exist.

Miracles

Reliable records substantiate Jesus' miracles. They were performed in public and were not denied by his enemies. Christ performed miracles before believers and skeptics alike, which was not the case with other so-called prophets or holy men. His miracles were also verified by the testimony of those he healed or otherwise rescued. These miracles demonstrated his various "super powers"

- over nature (calming the wind and sea, changing water to wine);
- over disease (healing lepers, the blind, and the lame)
- over demons (casting them out);
- over death (raising Lazarus, the ruler's daughter, and the son of the widow in Nain);
- with supernatural knowledge (such as prophecies);
- to create (feeding the thousands with a few loaves and fishes).

Arguably the most significant miracle of the Christian faith is that of Jesus' resurrection. Christ's body was buried in a stone tomb owned by Joseph of Arimathea (a member of the Sanhedrin sect that condemned Jesus). There were no competing burial stories, and it was recorded in writings too soon after the fact to have been a mere legend or myth.

The ancient writings of the apostles Mark and Paul confirm that there were eyewitnesses to this event. On the Sunday after Jesus' Good Friday crucifixion, his followers found the tomb empty. Various individuals and groups attest to numerous sightings of the risen Christ. These were confirmed by both friends and detractors of the faith. Jesus' disciples were thoroughly convinced of his resurrection, despite initially believing otherwise. Alternative explanations (such as the disciples stealing the body or that he didn't really die) were rejected for lack of credibility in the face of overwhelming evidence to the contrary. Thus, the biblical miracles demonstrate both the credibility of Jesus and the veracity of the Christian faith.

So what are miracles? C. S. Lewis wrote that miracles are "an interference with Nature by supernatural power."[14] Many of us would probably agree with this definition, but a scientific perspective can increase our understanding.

Various scholars have suggested that at least some miracles do not defy or break the laws of nature, but rather are miracles of timing, such as the parting of the Red Sea for the Israelites by powerful directional winds. Other miracles are perhaps evidence of higher natural laws that are beyond our current state of knowledge and understanding. As Jeff Greenberg, Wheaton College professor of geology, said, "Perhaps God is in the business of making the improbable probable."[15]

The uncertainties inherent in quantum mechanics create a space where, while perhaps quite improbable, pretty much anything is possible without violating the laws of physics. (Consider Schrödinger's probability cloud model of the atom: a nucleus of at least one proton and possibly one or more neutrons, surrounded by a fuzzy cloud where one or more electrons might be found; the denser the cloud, the more likely an electron is to be there, as opposed to the less dense parts of the cloud.)

In the late 1960s, string theory emerged in an attempt to unify the four physical forces of nature (electromagnetism, gravity, and the strong and weak nuclear forces). It bridges the incompatibility gap between quantum field theory (which ignores gravity, but works well at the subatomic particle level) and general relativity (which ignores quantum mechanics, but works well at larger scales). String theory replaces the notion of point-like subatomic particles with the concept of energetic vibrating strings, and predicts that our universe has possibly ten, eleven, or even twenty-six dimensions of space and time (time being one dimension; the rest being spatial) instead of the three dimensions of space and one dimension of time experienced in our day-to-day lives.

Based on the robust mathematical explanatory power of string theories, more recently physicists have been contemplating the idea that more dimensions of time might help move us closer to a grand unified theory (combining all the fundamental forces) as well.

Extra dimensions of space and time may put a whole new spin on how people think about miracles. For example, if God can move in two dimensions of time, rather than just the one forward-moving linear progression of time that humans experience, he can be everywhere at once. Similarly, extra dimensions of physical space would allow the various fundamental forces to act differently or even be suspended.

If fundamental forces like gravity or electromagnetic forces holding atoms and molecules together are temporarily suspended, then there is no need to think that when performing miracles, God is violating the very laws of physics that he ordained.

Paul Little wrote in his classic book, *Know Why You Believe*, "Miracles are not contrary to nature but only contrary to what we know about nature."[16]

Personal Experiences

Spiritual experiences also provide powerful evidence of God's existence to those who have had them. Scores of individuals throughout history and from all over the world have claimed that they have experienced God. While religious experiences can only constitute direct evidence of the veracity of Christianity for those privileged enough to have them, the fact that so many people testify to having had such experiences constitutes indirect evidence of Christianity even to those who have personally not had them.

Christian theologian and philosopher William Lane Craig said:

> God invaded my life when I was 16 years old, and for more than 30 years I've walked with him day by day, year by year, as a living reality in my experience. In the absence of overwhelming arguments for atheism—and in light of the powerful case for God and Christianity—it's perfectly rational to go on believing in the reality of that experience.[17]

No doubt many believers relate to Dr. Craig's testimony—I certainly can. In a personal journal, I keep a record of things I've been praying about: both good and bad. Whenever I need encouragement, all I have to do is go back and reflect on how time after time God has come through for me with direction and answers that have guided me forward.

From the big-picture perspective, his ways are far better than I could ever have imagined. From logic and reason, the sciences, moral law, and more, God has given me one evidence after another on which to build my beliefs.

In addition he has given me substantial evidence from his Word.

5 The Bible: Its Evidence, Interpretation, and Message

M<small>Y DESIRE HAS</small> always been to live an integrated life as both a good scientist and a faithful Christian. It never made sense to me that science and faith might be an "either/or" competition. If God truly is the Creator, then it just seems reasonable that he will reveal himself through his creation, and science is a powerful tool we can use to uncover those wonders. Properly practiced, science can be an act of worship in looking at God's revelation of himself in nature.

He also gave us his Word. To this day, the Bible remains one of the best-authenticated books in human history. Its

New Testament documents are unequivocally the best-authenticated writings of antiquity. That's true in terms of both the total number of manuscripts as well as the short span of time between their original authorship and the dates of the earliest manuscripts.

Noted Jewish archaeologist Nelson Glueck said, "In my opinion, every book of the New Testament was written between the forties and eighties of the First Century A.D."[1]

Biblical archaeologist W. F. Albright backs this up, stating, "We can already say emphatically that there is no longer any solid basis for dating any book of the New Testament after 80 A.D."[2] Fragments of copies of the New Testament books have been found dated from within fifty to one hundred years after the originals were written, validating his comment. Full copies have been found dated within three hundred to four hundred years of the originals.

In contrast, the earliest manuscripts of the classical histories of Tacitus, Caesar, Thucydides, Herodotus, and Livy are dated from 350 to 1,350 years after the time of the original writings. That's long enough for distortions to set in, yet their validity doesn't seem to be in question.

Authors of the Gospel accounts were either eyewitnesses to Jesus' life, or their close associates. Sir William Ramsay,

Scottish archaeologist and New Testament scholar, extolled the work of one particular Gospel writer, saying: "Luke is a historian of the first rank; not merely are his statements of fact trustworthy, he is possessed of the true historic sense . . . In short, this author should be placed along with the greatest of historians."[3]

If the Gospel writers had strayed from the facts, hostile witnesses who were still alive would have exposed them. As mentioned previously, Jesus' resurrection was confirmed by multiple witnesses. Various scholars point out that the disciples were willing to go to their deaths proclaiming that Jesus had risen from the dead. Surely no one would willingly die for a lie.

In addition to the powerful testimonies that substantiated these historic events, the New Testament reveals dozens of fulfilled prophecies about the Messiah, as well as the many historically confirmed miracles.

Multiple manuscripts of Old and New Testament documents exist with only insignificant variations among them. The manuscripts include more than four thousand written in Greek and thirteen thousand copies of portions of the New Testament. These numbers are orders of magnitude greater than the number of manuscripts of other classical historical documents, such as the writings of Caesar, Plato, and Sophocles.

The biblical texts were referenced and quoted as authoritative by ancient friends and foes of the faith alike. Seeing the fulfillment of hundreds of its predictions also satisfies my analytical mind. So does its historical corroboration with other sources.

Furthermore, criteria for inclusion in the New Testament canon included the following:

- The books must have been authored by apostles or close associates.
- The books had to be widely accepted by the churches.
- The teachings had to be in conformity with sound doctrine taught by the churches.

The Bible is truly a one-of-a-kind document. It was written over a 1,500-year span, by over forty authors who were able to maintain harmony and consistency. It has survived throughout many centuries in spite of periods of great persecution for those who have claimed it to be true. This book has had a profound influence on humankind and society. The fact that history and archaeology verify its accuracy should indicate to its readers that the more abstract ethical and moral teachings are accurate as well. The Bible is unlike any other book ever written, suggesting that the driving force behind it is also unique.

Sir Frederic Kenyon, British paleographer and biblical scholar, wrote, "No fundamental doctrine of the Christian faith rests on a disputed reading . . . It cannot be too strongly asserted that in substance the text of the Bible is certain."[4]

When measured against other classical literature, the historical reliability of the Bible is unrivaled. More than five thousand ancient handwritten copies exist. And so do close to twenty-five thousand copies of ancient manuscripts in all languages. The *Iliad* by Homer has the second-best documentation, but with less than seven hundred ancient texts in existence, it wanes in comparison to the support for the biblical texts.[5]

Such evidence led Frederick Bruce, former professor of biblical criticism and exegesis at the University of Manchester, to state:

> The evidence for our New Testament writings is ever so much greater than the evidence for many writings of classical authors, the

authenticity of which no one dreams of questioning. And if the New Testament were a collection of secular writings, their authenticity would generally be as beyond all doubt.[6]

Solid evidence—as a scientist, I like that.

To read the Bible, however, and gain the most accurate understanding requires some homework. Cracking open the Bible and reading whatever I find there from a contemporary Western perspective isn't enough. The context, the culture, the genre, the authorship, and the original audience have to be studied in order to comprehend the author's intent. By taking all these aspects together, it's easy to see that first and foremost, the Bible communicates a theological message. Perhaps the most important part of that message is the redemption of all God's creation through Jesus.

So Who Is Jesus?

Jesus Christ is arguably the most world-changing figure in the entirety of human history.[7] Author Paul Little wrote: "His arrival on earth split time in two . . . It changed the world's calendar and altered its mores."[8] Jesus has been the subject of more literature, art, and music than any other person.

So, why does Jesus seem to have such a permanent place in contemporary culture? Why does he seem as relevant today as he was two thousand years ago? Why is he still the topic of so many ongoing conversations? Why hasn't he faded into the past as many other great figures in history have? In spite of his unique status, Jesus is often lumped into the same group of great moral teachers as Buddha, Confucius, Gandhi, Mohammed, and others.

How do you see him? You might have gotten some of your ideas about Jesus from childhood Sunday school stories, or from one of the plethora of "Jesus" films. Perhaps the idea of him as a great teacher sounds good, and doesn't offend anyone. But is that all he was?

Most of what we know about Jesus comes from the Bible's New Testament, a collection of eyewitness memoirs, historical accounts, and letters written by his followers. Secular historians confirm much of it. The New Testament writings record many of the things Christ did and said, as well as offer a glimpse into the early years of Christianity. The same followers who wrote about his life also recorded that Jesus rose from the dead, and that he claimed to be God.

Author C. S. Lewis called the incarnation of God in the person of Jesus, "myth become fact."[9] Many myths of the ancient world refer to the story of a god who came down from heaven. Just like the stories of Adam and Eve in the Garden of Eden or of Noah's Great Flood appear in many different cultures, something like the God-Man story does too. Just as with eyewitnesses recounting any public event, the more people who tell a similar story, the more likely it is to be true.

Various possibilities have been suggested over the last two thousand years. They all boil down to a handful of basic options: legend, liar, lunatic, or Lord. Or, put another way: myth, mystic, menace, madman, or Messiah.

Both Jesus and his followers made claims about his godhood. In John 14:9 Jesus said, "He who has seen Me has seen the Father" (NKJV). He also said, "I and the Father are one" (John 10:30). In this account, Jesus claimed that he and God the Father are the same. This claim offended the Jews, and Jesus didn't try to take it back or deny it. Soon after he said this, the Jews picked up rocks to stone him, basically saying that they intended to stone him "for blasphemy, because you, a mere man, claim to be God" (10:33).

In another passage Jesus said, "I tell you the truth . . . before Abraham was born, I am!" (John 8:58). Although it might sound strange to our ears, to the Jews, the words *I am* are equivalent to "God." So, Jesus spoke and claimed God's sacred name, the name of the great "I am," the eternal ultimate reality personified in God the Father, the Holy Spirit, and in Jesus Christ. The Jews threatened to stone him again after he said this, and once again, he didn't deny the implications.

In John 11:25, he said, "I am the resurrection and the life. He who believes in me will live, even though he dies." Here Jesus is claiming to have the ability to save his followers from death, forever. Again and again Jesus points people to himself, unlike Buddha (for example) who said, "Be lamps unto yourselves."

The claims of his followers also shed some light on Christ's identity. In Mark 8:29, he asked his disciples point-blank, "Who do you say that I am?" To which the apostle Peter responded, "You are the Christ" (NASB). Jesus never corrected Peter. Had Jesus been an angel or a prophet, he would have been quick to explain that mistake.

The disciples claimed to see and touch Jesus after his resurrection, as well as to eat and drink with him. In John 20:28, when Thomas first saw Jesus after his resurrection, Thomas exclaimed, "My Lord and my God." Once again, Jesus let that truth stand.

Jesus' disciple John wrote: "In the beginning was the Word, and the Word was with God, and the Word was God"

(John 1:1). In verse 14, John continued: "The Word became flesh and made his dwelling among us." So, according to the laws of logic: if the Word who became flesh is Jesus, and the Word is God, then Jesus is God.

In addition to Jesus' and his followers' claims that he was God, in the apostle Paul's letter to the Colossian church, Jesus was identified as the Creator: "For by Him all things were created that are in heaven and that are on earth" (Colossians 1:16 NKJV). John the disciple confirmed this in his Gospel: "Through him all things were made; without him nothing was made that has been made" (John 1:3).

Jesus identified himself in the most-authenticated documents of antiquity. There was not enough time for myths or legends to develop before the biblical accounts were actually recorded. Authors of the Gospel accounts were either eyewitnesses of Jesus' life or close associates of them. If the Gospel writers had strayed from the facts, unfriendly witnesses would have jumped at the chance to expose them.

Even the secular press of the ancient world conceded these observations about Jesus:

1. He was a wise and moral teacher from Judea.
2. He performed miracles.

3. Jewish leaders condemned him for what they called sorcery and heresy.

4. He was crucified by Pontius Pilate at the Jewish Passover during the reign of Emperor Tiberius.

5. Christ's followers reported that he had risen from the dead.

6. The Christian faith spread to Rome, where adherents were so convinced that Jesus was God that they endured strong persecution.

7. First-century Christians worshiped Jesus as God and regularly reenacted the Lord's Supper.

C. S. Lewis eloquently summarizes Christ's identity in his iconic book, *Mere Christianity*:

> I am trying here to prevent anyone saying the really foolish thing that people often say about Him: I'm ready to accept Jesus as a great moral teacher, but I don't accept his claim to be God . . . Either this man was, and is, the Son of God, or else a madman or something worse. You can shut him up for a fool, you can spit at him and kill him as a demon or you can fall at his feet and call him Lord and God, but

let us not come with any patronizing nonsense about his being a great human teacher . . . Now it seems to me obvious that He was neither a lunatic nor a fiend: and consequently, however strange or terrifying or unlikely it may seem, I have to accept the view that He was and is God.[10]

As a scientist and a spiritual being, this preponderance of evidence has convinced me that Jesus and his followers told the truth. He is truly who he claimed to be—the Son of God, our Savior, and the Creator.

It was so from the very beginning.

6 Genesis and Origins: A Spectrum of Views

PEOPLE HOLD A multitude of views on the origins of the cosmos and life. Some believe that science and religion are always and forever at odds with each other. Many, like me, believe both science and religion offer ways to search for order and purpose in life.

Both disciplines consider life's big questions. Science is concerned with observations, experiments, and interpretation of the various phenomena of nature. Religion, on the other hand, is concerned with our fundamental beliefs about the source, purpose, and meaning of existence. Human intuition, faith, and reason are the means we use to move from observations and experiments to fundamental beliefs.[1]

Throughout the ages, prominent scientists and philosophers have offered valuable perspectives on the ways science and religion fit together:

- Moses Maimonides, Jewish philosopher, 1190: "Study astronomy and physics if you desire to comprehend the relation between the world and God's management of it."[2]

- Max Planck, Anglican churchwarden, atomic physicist, 1900s: "There can never be any real opposition between religion and science, for one is the complement of the other."[3]

- Henry Fritz Schaefer, Christian educator, chemist, 1991: "The significance and joy in my science comes in the occasional moments of discovering something new and saying to myself, 'So that's how God did it!' My goal is to understand a little corner of God's plan."[4]

- Even the self-proclaimed agnostic and pantheist-sympathizer Albert Einstein, author of the theory of relativity, circa 1941, made these statements: "Religion without science is blind. Science without religion is lame . . . I want to know God's thoughts; the rest are details."[5]

So, you might ask, where is the conflict? In the wake of Charles Darwin's work and writings on biological origins, scientists and philosophers began making statements such as this one from British biologist and humanist Sir Julian Huxley: "The earth was not created, it evolved. So did all the animals and plants that inhabit it, including our human selves, mind and soul as well as brain and body. So did religion."[6]

At the other end of the spectrum, Christian apologists such as Dr. Henry Morris have made statements like this:

> Divine revelation from the Creator of the world states that he did it all in six days several thousand years ago. The Bible contains all the basic principles upon which true science is built. There is no proven scientific evidence that the earth is old. There is no evidence whatever that evolution of one kind of organism into a more complex organism has ever occurred. Satan himself is the originator of the concept of evolution.[7]

71

These two extreme, polarized positions gave rise to a perceived contradiction between science (portrayed as endorsing evolution, atheism, and humanist ethics) on the one hand, and religion (portrayed as endorsing young-earth creation, God, and biblical ethics) on the other. The actual divide is between "Scientism" (a combination of unquestioning adherence to natural science and an atheistic worldview) and a form of "Creationism" (a combination of a Christian worldview and a strict biblical literalism, especially with regard to a relatively recent six-day creation). Both Scientism and Creationism represent "fundamentalist" positions in that adherents do not think critically about their own views, even in the light of contrary evidence.

So What's the Reality?

As the previous chapters have shown, this contradiction is not real. Rather it is a false impression or confusion of concepts that don't necessarily go together. In other words, many reputable scientists successfully practice science without an atheistic worldview. At the same time many Christians adhere to Scripture without a relatively recent six-day interpretation of creation.

Furthermore, many practicing scientists profess belief in a personal God. The results of a poll on this topic were published in the scientific journal *Nature* in 1997. Of scientists polled, 40% responded affirmatively to the following two statements:

1. I believe in a God in intellectual and emotional communication with humankind, i.e., a God to whom one may pray in expectation of receiving an answer. By "answer" I mean more than the subjective psychological effect of prayer.
2. I believe in continuation of the person after death into another world. [8]

Perhaps equally important, both Catholic and Protestant religious leaders have made statements acknowledging the compatibility of science and faith. Pope John Paul II said:

> Sacred Scripture wishes simply to declare that the world was created by God, and in order to teach this truth it expresses itself in the terms of the cosmology in use at the time of the writer. The Sacred Book likewise wishes to

tell men that the world was not created as the seat of the gods, as was taught by other cosmogonies and cosmologies, but was rather created for the service of man and the glory of God. Any other teaching about the origin and make-up of the universe is alien to the intentions of the Bible, which does not wish to teach how heaven was made but how one goes to heaven.[9]

More recently, Pope Francis announced, "God is not a demiurge or a magician, but the Creator who gives being to all entities . . . Evolution in nature is not opposed to the notion of creation, because evolution presupposes the creation of beings that evolve."[10] In the same speech, he noted that the Big Bang theory does not contradict the role of a divine Creator. Evangelical leader Billy Graham stated that:

The Bible is not a book of science. The Bible is a book of Redemption, and of course I accept the Creation story. I believe that God did create the universe. I believe God created humanity. Whether it came by an evolutionary process and at a certain point he took this person or being and made him a living soul or not, does not change the fact that God did create humanity. Whichever way God did it makes no difference as to what men and women are and their relationship to God.[11]

So the perceived gulf between science and Christianity is simply fictitious. Many organizations exist for the sole purpose of fostering the dialogue between science and Christianity. From the world of religion, we have Pope John Paul II and Pope Francis accepting the potential of evolution, and Billy Graham having an open mind toward it.

Christianity is about belief in Jesus Christ as Creator, Savior, and Lord, while science (properly practiced) is about observations and experiments leading to scientific hypotheses, theories, and mathematically formulated laws. Let's take, for example, the scientific observation that a living cell is only 1/1000 of an inch long, yet it contains about one meter of DNA with enough information to fill thirty volumes of an encyclopedia. What does intuition, faith, and reason lead us to believe, based on this reality? Is the impression of design real or a delusion? Aside from what today is referred to as "Intelligent Design," the notion of design in nature (*teleos* in

Greek) dates back at least as far as Aristotle's era. This concept is the belief that beauty, complexity, and functionality in nature point to a purposeful Designer.

So How Did It All Start?

There are a handful of common positions that science-minded contemporary Christians, as well as others, take on issues of origins.

Young-Earth Creation, Progressive Creation, and Theistic Evolution

These three positions essentially agree on all the basic theological questions; their main disagreements stem from time frames and direct-versus-indirect divine action. The young-earth position insists that God's activity in the origins of both the inanimate universe and biological life is entirely through direct intervention in natural processes. Progressive creation stretches out the time frame from literal twenty-four-hour days to ages, and holds that God intervenes directly for the creation of various kinds of biological life, but indirectly ordains and sustains natural processes for the inanimate universe. Theistic evolution tends to adhere to indirect

God-ordained and sustained natural processes both for the inanimate universe as well as for biological life.

All three of these positions agree on five basic tenets of biblical theology:

1. God created the universe.
2. The universe is very good.
3. Humans bear God's image.
4. Humans have fallen into sin.
5. God atones for sin through Christ's sacrifice on the cross.

The author of the creation accounts in Genesis (the first book of the Bible) used ancient near-Eastern science and ancient poetic prose to describe the world God created. The writer used imagery reflecting the science of the time, that of a three-tiered universe. The heavenly realm was pictured above the solid, dome-shaped firmament that held up the waters above the earth's atmosphere. It separated the waters above from the waters below. In contrast, try to imagine if God had inspired the author of Genesis to write in terms of today's science—with dark energy, dark matter, and genetic codes—let alone the science of our future! No early reader of the Genesis passages would have understood any of these references.

The ancient poetry approach to interpreting these creation passages refers to the structure of Genesis chapter 1, with its repetitive use of the word *day*. Days one through three each speak of "separating" and thereby creating spaces:

- first, separating light from dark (creating day/night, heavens);
- second, separating the waters above from the waters below (creating sky/atmosphere, seas); and
- third, separating the water and land (creating dry land/continents).

Days four through six speak of "filling," or decorating the created spaces with the sun, moon, and stars for the heavens; then flying creatures for the skies and sea creatures for the seas; and finally land animals and humans for the dry land.

Just imagine watching God at work designing the universe, creating space itself, and planning this grand yet intricate, unfolding story!

Deism

This position holds that God is impersonal and does not intervene in the world at all. He always remains outside of space and time. Though God may ordain and sustain natural processes, he never enters the time-space realm in which humans reside. This view of God is often referred to as the "God of the philosophers" position.

Atheism

Those who hold to this position don't believe in any kind of supernatural being or activity. Less than 5% of the world's population would classify themselves as true atheists.

Key Points on Origins

Evolution is not synonymous with atheism. And belief in creation by God is not synonymous with young-earth creationism. Also, it's important to recognize the role of faith in moving from scientific findings to personal beliefs. Everyone has faith of some kind (whether in God, naturalism, or scientism) that influences their interpretation of the world and the way things work.

It may be useful to move beyond the evolution-versus-creation debate. Recognizing that there is a full spectrum of positions (none of which has all the answers to every question nor holds the "right" position on the really important questions of life) would foster unity and constructive dialogue.

God's Revelation Through Scripture and Science

Further exploration of the "two books" concept of God's revelation shows us even more of *who* he is. Galileo, Saint Augustine, Francis Bacon, and other key figures throughout history have affirmed that God is the author of both the Bible and nature. Various passages of Scripture reflect this view.

In the Old Testament, King David wrote, "The heavens are telling the glory of God; and the firmament proclaims his handiwork. Day to day pours forth speech, and night to night declares knowledge" (Psalm 19:1–2 NRSV).

In the New Testament, Saint Paul wrote in his letter to the Romans that, "For since the creation of the world God's invisible qualities—his eternal power and divine nature—have been clearly seen, being understood from what has been made, so that men are without excuse" (1:20). The commentators for *The New Interpreter's Study Bible* convey that this verse assures us that creation gives everyone on Earth a basic knowledge of God. Likewise, King David's passage portrays the universe as "sounding forth a liturgy of praise" to the Creator.[12]

Surely people everywhere can learn at least something about the Creator by studying his handiwork. And the more we learn, the more we see his glory—that's what makes science so fascinating.

A proper understanding of the relationship between science and the Christian faith allows them to complement, rather than contradict each other. Article 2 of the Belgic Confession states:

> Moreover, we know God by two means, first, by the creation, preservation, and government of this whole world. For it is before our eyes as a most beautiful Book in which all creatures, from the least to the greatest, are as certain letters and marks through which the invisible things of God can be examined and understood, certainly His eternal power and His divinity as the Apostle Paul says in Romans 1:20. This knowledge is sufficient for convicting any given people and rendering them inexcusable. But He also bears His very self to us, much

more clearly and openly, in His holy and divine Word; indeed, as much as is expedient in this life for His glory and for the salvation of His own people.[13]

Sir Francis Bacon, father of inductive reasoning (and at least partially responsible for developing the scientific method), was a contemporary of the Belgic Confession's authors and is often credited with the origin of the "God's two books" analogy.[14] These books of creation and the Bible are sometimes respectively referred to as general and special revelation. If our perfect and truthful God is the author of them both, then logically they cannot contradict each other.

We might want to take Sir Francis Bacon's exhortation as our own:

> Let no woman or man, out of conceit or laziness, think or believe that anyone can search too far or be too well informed in the Book of God's Words or the Book of God's Works: religion or science. Instead, let everyone endlessly improve their understanding of both.[15]

We may also want to consider Pascal's Wager, wherein seventeenth-century French mathematician Blaise Pascal asserted the following:

1. If you erroneously believe in God, you lose nothing (that is, death is the end for everyone, but you've lived a virtuous life);

2. If you correctly believe in God, you gain everything (eternal bliss in heaven with God).

3. Conversely, if you correctly disbelieve in God, you gain nothing (death being the end);

4. But if you erroneously disbelieve in God, you lose everything (that is, eternal separation from God).

So, as Pascal asserts, regardless of whether God's existence can be proven, the best bet is to believe. The Goldilocks Principle, as described in chapter 7, weights that bet even more in God's favor.

7 The Goldilocks Principle: Just-Right for Life

A BEAUTIFUL BLUE MARBLE in space—home to seven billion people (including you)—Planet Earth is right in the sweet spot of our solar system, the Goldilocks Zone. It's not too hot, and it's not too cold. Tilted perfectly at 23.5 degrees, Earth spins on its axis once every twenty-four hours while revolving around the sun at about 67,000 miles an hour.

As a physical scientist, the teleological fine-tuning argument especially intrigues me. It fascinates many others, too, as perhaps the most common argument for God's existence in today's technology-fixated society. Quoted in a *Los Angeles Times* newspaper article, modern-day science historian Frederic Burnham said that the idea that God created the universe is "a more respectable hypothesis today than at any time in (the) last hundred years."[1]

Associated with great thinkers from Plato and Aristotle to Saint Thomas Aquinas and William Paley, this teleological argument claims that the design and order observed in the natural realm point to a purposeful Creator.[2] Scientists and observers alike are perpetually amazed by the intricacy and complexity of our cosmos and the life it supports. Yet all of its details fit together impeccably in a perfectly balanced, synergistic system. As we study the complexity of the cosmos—from the tiniest atom to the frontiers of the universe—we quickly realize that chance can't explain its incredible order and elegance.

Even though possibly 10% or more of sun-like stars in the universe could support planetary systems, and thousands of extra-solar planets have already been detected, our exploration efforts so far have not revealed any other places in the universe quite like Earth.

Planet Earth's most blatant distinctive fact is that it's inhabited. The Old Testament prophet Isaiah remarked: "For thus says the LORD, who created the heavens (he is God!), who formed the earth and made it (he established it; he did not create it a chaos, he formed it to be inhabited!): I am the LORD, and there is no other" (Isaiah 45:18 NRSV).

Earth's unique attributes make it not only habitable, but also hospitable. Observers can easily see an arrangement and coordination of details that could not have happened by accident. Only a Master Designer had the power and wisdom to design and construct this planet to be inhabited.

Despite speculations to the contrary, exploration of our local space neighborhood confirms that the other planets in our solar system are not even close to being capable of sustaining life forms of any complexity. In comparison to Earth, the other objects in our solar system are wastelands. Earth's so-called sister planet, Venus, is a rocky terrestrial planet just slightly smaller than Earth and a little closer to the sun, but that's as far as their similarities go. Venus has a surface temperature of about 900°F and an atmosphere of carbon dioxide so thick that its atmospheric pressure is more than ninety times that of Earth. Its clouds are laced with sulfuric acid, and there's no water.

In the other direction we have another rocky terrestrial planet, Mars, which is significantly smaller than Earth and a little farther from the sun. Mars has very little atmosphere, and its only water is frozen, so there is no life-giving water cycle.

No Place Like Home

In *The Remarkable Spaceship Earth*, author Ron Cottrell points out nine specific attributes of Earth that make it habitable.[3] This book was the first I ever read as a young person that pointed out the amazing fine-tuning of Earth's capacity for life. A few years ago I had the privilege of meeting Cottrell and letting him know how his book inspired me. Another of my astronomer friends, Mark Ritter,[4] has helped me further flesh out Cottrell's original list of Earth's attributes and their complex, interdependent relationships with the various parts of our biosphere. Our three-way collaboration resulted in the following list of Earth's finely tuned characteristics:

1. *Earth's Distance from the Sun*
   - If Earth's distance from the sun were just 5% smaller, the atmospheric greenhouse effect would raise surface temperatures to 900°F, similar to what can be seen on Venus.
   - If the Earth-sun distance were just 1% greater, Earth would experience a continual Ice Age.

- Our sun itself is a very stable star, even among other G-class stars. Its energy and heat output only vary over time by +/- 0.1%, rather than the inhospitable average variance of +/- 4% for its fellow G-class family members.

2. *Earth's Size (Weight and Diameter)*

- If Earth's weight and diameter were greater, our planet's core temperature would be hotter, which would increase surface temperatures. Earth's gravity and atmospheric pressure would also be greater, with more of the lightweight dangerous gases (such as methane and ammonia) being retained. Depending on the amount of increase, life would be at the very least threatened, if not altogether impossible.

- If Earth's weight and diameter were smaller, its gravity would be weaker, and our atmosphere (including our essential water vapor and much of our oxygen) would be too light to be retained. In addition, decreased surface temperatures would result in a wasteland similar to what can be seen on Mars.

- The deadly gases methane (CH_4) and ammonia (NH_3) have molecular weights of 16 and 17 grams per mole respectively and are fortunately too light to stay in our atmosphere for very long, while life-giving water vapor (H_2O) at 18 grams per mole is just barely heavy enough!

- Interestingly, the weight of molecular oxygen, also vital for life, is 32 grams per mole. But oxygen is only that heavy because it predominantly exists in our atmosphere as a diatomic molecule (O_2; two atoms stuck together). Otherwise its weight would only be 16 grams per mole, and, like methane, it would not be heavy enough to stay in our atmosphere for very long!

3. *Earth's Atmosphere*

- Earth's atmosphere viewed from space has been described as a "thin blue line" because it appears almost insignificant next to the earth.
- Yet our atmosphere insulates us from the extreme day-to-night temperature ranges in space.
- It also protects us from harmful solar and cosmic radiation.
- The ozone layer in our stratosphere further protects us by absorbing high-energy radiation from space.

- If there were less ozone in our stratosphere, biological life would be destroyed by the excess radiation.

- If there were more ozone in the stratosphere, biological life would not receive enough of the sun's energy for photosynthesis and vitamin D synthesis.

- Our atmosphere's composition is perfect, with 78% nitrogen, 21% oxygen, 1% argon, and other trace gases. Just a little more or less of either nitrogen or oxygen would ultimately result in death.

- The small amount of carbon dioxide in the atmosphere is just enough to hold in some heat, but not enough to create a runaway greenhouse effect.

- The small percentage of water vapor in our atmosphere also helps hold in some heat. In addition, that just-right water vapor provides us with rain as a vital part of Earth's water cycle.

- On average, lightning strikes somewhere on Earth once each second. More than that and we'd have too many grass and forest fires. Less than that and not enough nitrogen from the atmosphere would get converted into the nitrates essential for plant growth.

4. *Earth's Magnetic Field*

- Our magnetic field protects us by repelling charged particles from the solar wind, which might otherwise tear Earth's atmosphere away, molecule by molecule.

- The small amount of solar wind that creeps through the magnetic field at Earth's north and south poles produce the aurorae, which serve as beautiful reminders of how the magnetic field protects us.

- Migratory animals such as honeybees, butterflies, homing pigeons, tuna, and dolphins all have magnetite in their brains. This substance acts like a compass needle, enabling these animals to sense the orientation of Earth's magnetic field and make their seasonal migrations northward and southward within it.

5. *Earth's Twenty-Four-Hour Rotation Rate*

- A slower daily rotation rate would cause longer days, during which plant life could burn up, and longer nights, during which plant life could freeze.

- A faster daily rotation rate would drastically alter Earth's climates: the tropics would get warmer while the poles would get colder, reducing the livable areas and possibly bringing about another Ice Age.

6. *Earth's Axial Tilt*
   • The 23.5° tilt of Earth's north-south polar axis as it re-volves around the sun gives us seasons and actually doubles the available crop-growing land area.

7. *Earth's Only Natural Satellite (Our Moon)*
   • The moon not only helped ancient people keep track of time, but it also is largely responsible for our ocean tides.
   • If the moon were bigger or much closer, it would cause tidal waves, submerging continents on a regular basis.
   • If this natural satellite were smaller or much farther away, there would be no tides and shoreline waters would quickly stagnate.
   • The moon is also just the right size to stabilize Earth's rotation axis at a 23.5° tilt, as well as to maintain Earth's rotation rate at twenty-four hours per day.
   • If the earth had more (or less) than one moon, our tides, daily rotation rate, and tilt would all be affected.

8. *Earth's Crust*

- Earth's geological crust ranges from four miles thick in ocean basins to thirty miles thick under some mountain peaks.

- Yet if the earth's crust were just ten to twenty feet thicker, the metallic elements within the crust would have combined with all the free oxygen in the atmosphere, making it unavailable to support life.

- Conversely, if the earth's crust were any thinner, it would be more fragile, and there would be much more seismic and volcanic activity.

9. *Earth's Liquid Water*

- Earth is the only known place in the universe to have liquid water and the water cycle necessary for life. Simply put, without water, there is no life. Instead, there are only wastelands.

- Water is a basic building block and perfect solvent for the other chemicals needed for life. Probably the most important compound on Earth, water's relatively low boiling point allows it to be easily purified on an ongoing basis as part of Earth's life-sustaining water cycle.

- Another important, though bizarre, property of water is that, unlike other substances, it becomes less dense when it freezes and floats on top of liquid water, acting as an insulating blanket. Without this strange characteristic, it would act like other liquids, becoming denser and sinking as it freezes, allowing more ice to form on top of the surface. In this scenario, rivers, lakes, and oceans would freeze essentially solid during the winter. In the summer, only the top of the ice would melt. Earth's water would exist as masses of solid ice with seasonal surface slush, making biological life virtually impossible.

Out of This World

The rest of our solar system also bears the marks of design. Saturn and Jupiter, gas giants in the outer region of the solar system, are close enough to protect us from incoming Earth-bound comets and asteroids, but not so close as to disturb our perfect but fragile orbit around the sun. And our star, the sun, is the perfect size, brightness, and age for life. Most stars have at least one other companion. Fortunately our sun appears to be a single star. If it had a nearby stellar partner, our orbit would destabilize, and Earth would ultimately crash into one or the other of our stars. Change anything, and life disappears.

Furthermore, the location of our solar system within the Milky Way Galaxy is ideal for life. We are far from the densely crowded, high-radiation, productive star-forming region closer to the center, in a safer open space between two spiral arms, yet not so far toward the outer edge of the galaxy to lack the heavy elements necessary for a terrestrial planet and life.

Powerful evidence of this life-friendly design can be seen not just here in our solar system and galactic location, but throughout the entire universe. For example:

- If the velocity of light were faster, too much radiation would reach Earth. If it were slower, we couldn't see and study as many stars.

- If the electromagnetic force were either stronger or weaker, chemical bonding would be dramatically altered, and we wouldn't have the right elements and compounds available for life.

- If the strong nuclear force were stronger or good for longer distances, all the protons and neutrons in the universe would be stuck together in one gigantic mass.

- If the strong nuclear force were weaker, we'd have no other atoms than hydrogen.

- If the expansion rate of the universe were slower or the mass density greater or the gravitational constant greater, the universe would have collapsed back into itself.

- If the expansion rate of the universe were faster or the mass density lower or the gravitational constant smaller, stars and planets would never have formed.

But Wait, There's More!

Another obvious place where amazing complexity is observed is in biology. Just a single living cell contains as much information as 100 million pages from an encyclopedia. Sir Fred Hoyle estimated the odds of getting just the basic enzymes together that are necessary for life (never mind the DNA, or an actual cell) to be 1 chance in $10^{40,000}$ power![5] Most statisticians would assert that probabilities of anything less than 1 chance in 10^{50} power are statistically impossible. So the odds of getting just the basic enzymes together for life are unfathomably remote.

Earth's early atmosphere would not have allowed even the basic building blocks of life to develop because there was no ammonia, methane, or hydrogen available. Baylor University scientist and professor Walter Bradley expresses the problem of life coming about spontaneously on Earth:

> The mathematical odds of assembling a living organism are so astronomical that nobody still believes that random chance accounts for the origin of life . . . Even if you optimized the conditions, it wouldn't work. If you took all the carbon in the universe and put it on the face of the earth, allowed it to chemically react at the most rapid rate possible, and left it for a billion years, the odds of creating just one functional protein molecule would be one chance in 10 with 60 zeroes after it.[6]

Someone might object, "All of this just pertains to life as we know it! What if there is a different kind of life that can survive in other conditions?" Well, given the laws of physics that seem to operate consistently throughout the entire universe, our kind of carbon-based life is the only kind of life this universe could produce and support. As an interesting side note, all the elements that make up your body (except for hydrogen, which was around even before the stars!)—from the carbon in your cells to the calcium in your teeth and bones to the iron in your blood—were forged in the fiery furnaces of stars and stellar explosions. Quite literally, we are made of "star-stuff"! How cool is that?

Both English theologian William Paley and naturalist Charles Darwin, who was born just four years after Paley's death, marveled at the complexity of the eye. Paley pointed out the "fitting together efficiently and cooperatively of the lens, retina and brain, enabling humans to have vision, as conclusive evidence of the design of an all-wise Creator. Thus the functional design of organisms and their features are taken as evidence of the existence of the Designer."[7]

Charles Darwin is listed by author Martin Marty (and others) as one of four "god-killers." The other three so defamed by Marty and his colleagues are Karl Marx, the father of communism; Friedrich Nietzsche, self-proclaimed anti-Christ and "killer of God"; and Sigmund Freud, who with Darwin promoted the view that humans were merely the smartest animals, not otherwise distinct from them.[8] Yet Darwin himself never claimed to be an atheist and remained an active parish worker for most of his life. He struggled, as many do, with the problem of reconciling evil in the world (particularly the suffering he observed in nature) with a good and benevolent view of God.

Many great thinkers throughout human history have argued that design requires a designer. When we contemplate a beautiful building, a spaceship, or a work of fine art, we don't think these things happened by accident. Why would we think the significantly more complex universe or any living thing was any less purposefully designed?

Virtually all astronomers and astrophysicists of the current era recognize the Anthropic Cosmological Principle laid out by J. D. Barrow and F. J. Tipler in 1986. It represents the thesis that there is a long and growing list of universal attributes whose magnitudes must fall within a very narrow range of values in order for life to exist on Earth.[9] Many of these attributes apply to the universe at large and, therefore, to the possibility of life existing anywhere within it. This concept is also known as the Goldilocks Principle: none of these values are too big or too small; they are all just right. The number of attributes included on the list ranges by investigator from dozens to hundreds, and the calculated odds of getting each attribute's value "just right" also varies quite widely between estimators. A probability estimation of 1 chance in $10^{\wedge}250^{th}$ power is probably pretty close to the middle of the pack. Want to see what that number looks like?

10,000,000,000,000,000,000,000,000,000,000,
000,000,000,000,000,000,000,000,000,000,00
0,000,000,000,000,000,000,000,000,000,000,0
00,000,000,000,000,000,000,000,000,000,000,
000,000,000,000,000,000,000,000,000,000,00
0,000,000,000,000,000,000,000,000,000,000,
000,000,000,000,000,000,000,000,000,000,00
0,000,000,000,000,000,000,000,000,000

It's really hard for us mere humans to comprehend what that number represents, but to put it in perspective, the odds of picking one particular atom from all the atoms in the universe is only 1 chance in $10^{\wedge}80^{th}$ power, and the odds of picking one particular atom from all the atoms in $10^{\wedge}80^{th}$ universes is still only 1 chance in $10^{\wedge}160^{th}$ power. Statisticians say that odds of anything beyond 1 chance in $10^{\wedge}50^{th}$ power are not just improbable, but rather impossible. In other words, it ain't gonna happen, unless it's rigged, and by "rigged," I mean designed that way.

The only real alternative to an intelligent Creator is that the entire natural realm came about by chance. But chance has no power to create order. And with the odds of all the many finely tuned characteristics of the universe coming together calculated at well beyond the threshold of statistical impossibility, chance is not a reasonable explanation. In the current scientific marketplace of ideas, the touch point for dialogue between science and theology comes down to a discussion of probabilities with theists pointing to the *teleos*, or purposeful design and the improbability of all we observe coming together by random chance. Conversely, atheists would like to improve the odds by providing more chances to get it all just right, but that doesn't really change anything.

So convincing and statistically improbable is the evidence of bio-friendliness in the universe that currently the only real argument countering the involvement of some type of creative intelligence is the multiverse hypothesis. This conjecture speculates that there may be an infinite number of separate universes, each with a different set of physical laws. Our universe is perhaps the only one among them to randomly get the set of physical laws just right so that life can exist. There is no real way as of yet to either verify or falsify the existence of additional parallel universes, so the multiverse hypothesis is currently untestable. But even if we allow speculation on the existence of additional universes, they still all rely on the existence of some set of orderly physical laws.[10]

With a similar sense of exasperation, scientists studying planetary formation to learn more about the bio-friendliness of conditions on the early earth are frustrated by the many environmental obstacles to chemical and prebiological evolution. The only real alternative to creative intelligence under serious consideration within the evolutionary biology community is the transpermia theory, which suggests that the building blocks for life (or possibly even actual cells) came to Earth from somewhere else in the cosmos. Again, this is pure speculation, and only transplants the problem of abiogenesis (the natural process of life arising from nonliving matter) to an unknown location that we have even less information about than the early earth.[11]

Renowned author and theoretical physicist Paul Davies wrote that

> the degree of bio-friendliness we observe in the universe seems far in excess of what is needed to give rise to a few observers . . . If the ingenious bio-friendliness of our universe were the result of randomness, we might

expect the observed universe to be minimally, rather than optimally, biophilic. Note too, that multiverse explanations still need to assume the existence of laws of some sort, so they do not offer a complete explanation of the law-like order of the universe. Finally, invoking an infinity of unseen universes to explain certain features of the universe we do observe seems the antithesis of Occam's Razor: It is an infinitely complex explanation.[12]

Randy Van Dragt, professor of biology at Calvin College, and James Clark, professor of geology at Wheaton College, wrote in an essay on environmental stewardship:

In Romans 8:19 Paul tells us that all of creation is looking forward to the salvation of God's people, for therein the creation itself will be relieved of the curse to which it was subjected through the fall of humankind. Personal salvation in Christ eventually translates to the redemption and restoration of all creation. This bears out God's redemptive intent expressed in John 3:16, where Jesus says, "For God so

loved the cosmos [all that He had made] that
He gave His only Son."[13]

Thus, Jesus was saying in John 3:16 that God loved the
entire universe and everything in it! As scientists continue to
study its complexity, from the most miniscule quark or lepton
to the dark energy fueling the expansion of the universe, it
becomes increasingly clear to me that God must truly love his
creation. The scale of the universe is beyond comprehension
to most of us, yet the more we learn about it, the more we realize that none of it is wasted space.

For me, science is the tool that can be used to explore
the natural realm and illuminate the characteristics of the
awesome God who formed atoms, time, energy, and space
out of nothing. He's the One who put it all together. The
teleological argument can indeed bear witness to God's
existence and divine attributes, perhaps especially for the
skeptical empiricist.

William Lazareth beautifully wrote for the Augustine
Institute that "the creation shows forth his wisdom and
power . . . Notwithstanding its inherent ambiguities, it bears
witness to God's steadfast love and care . . . The majesty of

God, reflected in the creation, is a reason for worshiping and thanksgiving, for trusting and obeying God."[14]

• •

Is God a Programmer?

Here's a thought experiment for you: What if God is like a masterful computer programmer with an end goal in mind: a free will–based relationship with independent, rational beings? He defines all the initial conditions (energy, matter, space, and time) of the universe, writes the code (the laws of nature), runs the program, and sustains the processes? Would you be more or less in awe of him than you currently are?

• •

Putting Order in Place

In 1650, Sir Isaac Newton asked, "Whence arises all that order and beauty we see in the world?"[15] What a great question!

Why *is* the universe beautiful, orderly, and understandable? What *about* the laws of nature? Where did they come from? In the Old Testament book of Jeremiah, the author wrote that God "established [his] covenant with day and night and the ordinances of heaven and earth" (33:25 NRSV). The physical laws collaboratively guiding interactions between matter, space, energy, and time may seem arbitrary, but they resulted in a highly ordered universe that provided the perfect conditions for life on our little blue planet.

Just try, for a moment, to imagine a universe without fixed physical laws. Without the lawful order that we observe, the universe would be absolutely chaotic and incomprehensible. We would not be able to study and learn about nature. There is no known reason why the physical laws that govern the universe must necessarily exist. For example, there are no inherent reasons why

- masses should attract each other as they do according to Newton's Law of Universal Gravity;
- large masses should bend space according to Einstein's Theory of Relativity;
- oppositely charged particles should attract each other, and similarly charged particles should repel each other according to Coulomb's Law;

- the flow of charged particles (electricity) should behave according to Ohm's Law;
- the strong nuclear force should be strong enough to overcome the electromagnetic repulsion between protons in holding them so close together in the nucleus of an atom, but should then suddenly become nonexistent beyond the edge of the nucleus.

The physical laws of nature seem capriciously dictated until we realize how synergistically they work together. This realization makes me reflect on Colossians 1:16–17, which reads, "For by Him all things were created, both in the heavens and on earth, visible and invisible, whether thrones or dominions or rulers or authorities—all things have been created through Him and for Him. He is before all things, and in Him all things hold together" (NASB).

In a mysterious way, we can say that Christ is the ordering power behind the physical laws. His power keeps the nucleus of every atom together, and holds the planets in orbit around the sun!

There's an old YouTube video of the 1971 Apollo 15 moon walk that shows when Commander David Scott performed a live demonstration of Galileo's prediction that, ignoring air friction, all objects fall at the same rate of gravitational acceleration regardless of their weight. This scientific premise discussed for centuries became a popular topic while the world watched on television as a feather and hammer dropped by Commander Scott hit the moon's surface at the same time. But *why* is there gravity?

So much in both realms of science and faith may not be fully understood for hundreds or thousands of years. My hope is that I never lose a holy curiosity about the way God works in either realm.

Lydia Jaeger, physicist and academic dean at l'Institut Biblique de Nogent-sur-Marne, wrote in her essay *Cosmic Order and Divine Word*:

> The "law"-like regularity and consequent modelability of natural phenomenon are the unquestioned assumptions that underlie all scientific research . . . But common to all except for the most extreme relativists is the conviction that there is some basic, deep order in Nature that allows for the emergence of meaningful scientific practice . . . This view and the refrain of ultimate goodness ("God saw all that He had made, and it was very good") stands in

clear contrast to the Babylonian imperial cosmology in which Creation results from warfare in a power struggle between competing gods . . . In particular, laws of Nature are not self-explanatory. To me, they are most powerfully interpreted as traces of the Creator's handwriting.[16]

The physical laws of nature—obvious whenever we look at Hubble Space Telescope images of galactic star nurseries or multiple images of the same star due to gravitational lensing—point to a Creator. He is a God of power, order, rationality, and care for creation who, according to the cause-and-effect logic of the cosmological argument, must exist outside and apart from the created realm of space, time, matter, and energy. At the very least, this much can be read from the Book of Nature.

The fact that we humans not only survive but rather thrive in our environment tells me that the Creator loves us deeply and lavishly. God might have created a world without vibrant colors (picture a glorious sunset, or those Hubble images), delicious flavors (imagine your favorite foods), and beautiful sounds (think of a waterfall or your favorite music). None of these are a necessity for survival, but rather the gifts of a generous Creator.

Even secular physicists such as Sir Fred Hoyle have made such comments as: "There is a coherent plan in the universe, though I don't know what it's a plan for."[17] The late British philosopher Antony Flew, who recently converted from atheism to theism, cited the motivation for his conversion as "reason, mainly in the form of arguments to design."[18]

The exquisite design of the universe from the Big Bang to its farthest reaches and its infinitesimal details is just right. Its physical laws point intelligent, spiritual creatures toward their loving Creator.[19] That means we ought to be taking good care of all he's given us.

8 Environmental Stewardship: This Is My Father's World

G ROWING UP NEAR a First Nations American Indian reservation in the Pacific Northwest, I revered my father, who was a forester as well as a Boy Scout wilderness leader. By watching him, I learned from a young age the importance of taking care of our surroundings. As soon as I turned fourteen, I started spending summers working in the forestry and fishing industries, and that continued until graduate school. Those early years cultivated a special and enduring closeness to nature. To this day, I still enjoy the great outdoors in every possible way, every chance I get!

That's why a few years ago, when Dr. Calvin DeWitt (one of the leading Christian environmentalists in the United States) asked me to join him as a founding member of the Academy of Evangelical Scientists and Ethicists working to promote environmental concern and creation care, I embraced the opportunity. By now, I've spent several years in this capacity contemplating the notion of a Christian environmental ethic and how to encourage others to intentionally consider their own values and beliefs relative to environmental issues. In doing so, perhaps Christ-followers can lead the way in learning to make wise decisions pertaining to the environment.

Unfortunately, however, it seems as if our culture is inundated with secular jargon regarding environmental issues. There's rhetoric about saving Mother Earth, the Gaia hypothesis, and the idea that the entire earth and everything on it is most properly viewed as a single organism. But what about our perspective as Christ-followers?

Perhaps our Father (the Creator) has a higher calling for us to be good caretakers of his creation—his lavish gift to us. In the same way as I learned from my father as a young girl, perhaps we can learn from our heavenly Father and each other how to develop a logical and cohesive mental framework from which to make important ethical decisions about the world we live in.

Seeing the Creator's Heart

Various Scripture verses speak of the value God puts on creation. There are two specific Bible passages that have had the greatest impact on my personal view of creation. The first is at the end of the first creation account in Genesis 1:31: "And God saw everything that he had made, and behold, it was very good" (RSV). If God viewed all that he had created and thought it was good, how much more should I respect and care for it?

The second very familiar passage is from John 3:16. Many Christians know this verse by heart: "For God so loved the world that he gave his only Son, that whoever believes in him should not perish but have eternal life" (RSV). The word translated "world" in our Bibles is actually the Greek word *cosmos*. That includes every created thing in the entire universe! Just think about what that means: God loved all of his creation so much that he sent his Son, Jesus, to die to reconcile it to himself! God deeply loves and values everything he made.

Matthew 6:21 adds insight to environmental concerns as well: "For where your treasure is, there will your heart be also" (RSV). With the price of petroleum fuels today, particularly at the gas pump, the threat to our wallets may sadly be the motivating factor that many of us need to actually do something about environmental conservation. Let's hope and pray that what we treasure most is not measured in financial terms, but rather by storing up treasures in heaven. And to do that, we need to care about the things God cares about in his creation.

Our Amazing Home

This planet where we reside is completely unique within our solar system. Among other things it supplies:

- ample water in all three physical phases
- a protective, insulating atmosphere
- a magnetic field that deflects dangerous charged particles from the solar wind
- the perfect mass, thus gravity, to hold on to ample amounts of oxygen and water vapor, but not much deadly methane and ammonia
- the perfect distance from the sun to provide temperate climates and adequate energy[1]

These components of the earth's crust, water, and atmosphere plus the physical, chemical, and biological processes that govern their interactions make up Earth's "biosphere" (the sphere around the earth, including its atmosphere, that supports life) and provides what human beings and all other organisms need not only to survive, but also to flourish and thrive. Presented with the physical life-giving attributes of this planet, our innately curious human minds inevitably ponder the bigger questions:

- To whom does this planet and its resources belong?
- What is the proper role of humans relative to the earth?
- How can humans live on the earth in synergy and peace with its other inhabitants in a long-term, sustainable way?

The Old Testament book of Ecclesiastes causes us to ponder a poetic yet accurate description of the earth's systems from a biblical perspective:

> The sun rises and the sun goes down, and
> hastens to the place where it rises. The wind

blows to the south, and goes round to the north; round and round goes the wind, and on its circuits the wind returns. All streams run to the sea, but the sea is not full; to the place where the streams flow, there they flow again (Ecclesiastes 1:5–7 RSV).

Earth's sun is the primary energy source for all of the earth's processes. The sun causes atmospheric winds to distribute heat and water vapor around the globe, controlling precipitation. It also powers the water cycle, distilling or purifying Earth's water through evaporation and humidifying the air with water vapor. Frozen water ice in the form of glaciers and ice sheets serves as a network of storage reservoirs, as well as planetary thermostats that reflect a portion of the sun's radiation back into space, and prevent the earth from overheating.

Biogeochemical processes (including the rock cycle and photosynthesis) recycle carbon, nitrogen, sulfur, phosphorus, oxygen, and other substances required for life. Photosynthesis is responsible for converting the sun's energy into chemical energy stored in plants, which is ultimately converted into the fossil fuel energy that the entire global economic system is so dependent upon.

Today, we (every single human being) are confronted with a number of threats to the creation that God blessed and called "good." Some of the major issues that are currently global concerns include:

- energy resources
- air pollution
- water resources
- climate change
- deforestation
- loss of biodiversity

Looking at each of these issues individually will help us better understand them.

Energy Resources and Air Pollution

At the present rate of energy consumption (nearly 9 trillion joules per second, or watts), all of the earth's fossil fuel energy (about 3.5×10^{22} joules)—much of it coal—will be consumed in about 120 years. American oil production peaked about 35 years ago, while global oil production is expected to peak within the next ten years.[2] Obviously our fossil fuel reserves aren't going to last forever.

Closely intertwined with our current dependence on fossil fuels are air quality issues. Of Earth's atmospheric gases, 80% are located within ten miles of Earth's surface. The "thin blue line" of our delicate atmosphere as seen from space is essential for our existence. However, the quantity of man-made pollutants (from industrial, agricultural, and automotive sources; all largely powered by fossil fuels) is now substantial enough to contaminate the atmosphere. This leads to air pollution and acid rain, with their negative effects on the health and well-being of not only humans, animals, and plants, but also on inanimate natural as well as manufactured objects.

Venus, our sister planet in the solar system, contains pretty close to the same amount of carbon as the earth. However, instead of the carbon being located predominantly in the ground as it is on Earth, it is located in Venus' atmosphere in the form of carbon dioxide, a potent greenhouse gas. Due to this large amount of atmospheric carbon dioxide, Venus' surface temperature is approximately 900°F. That's nearly twice as hot as Mercury, in spite of Mercury's position much closer to the sun! By extracting and burning fossil fuels here on Earth, we are in the process of moving carbon from the ground into the atmosphere. The resultant warming of Earth's atmosphere is obvious and undisputed among reputable climate scientists.[3]

The bottom line is that Earth's fossil fuels are not only limited and nonrenewable, but their use is also damaging Earth's delicately balanced biosphere in unsustainable ways. If current energy consumption rates continue—let alone increase with the growing global population and industrialization of developing countries—we must be able to effectively develop and utilize more renewable and, more importantly, sustainable energy sources such as solar, wind, geothermal, hydroelectric, or even safeguarded nuclear technologies.

Water Resources

The lack of abundant, easily accessible, and sustainable clean water sources in many locations around the world presents an extreme challenge for people who want to live long and healthy lives in these places. How many times have we all heard the old adage "waste not, want not"? When it comes to water, everyone needs to heed this advice.

For those who live in more developed countries, it's easy to take our water supplies and Earth's water cycle for granted; however, only 3% of Earth's total water supply is fresh, and more than two-thirds of that fresh water is frozen. More than 30% of Earth's total fresh water (0.9% of Earth's total supply) is in the ground, leaving only about 0.3% of the fresh water

(0.009% of Earth's total supply) unfrozen and available at the surface, which is the water used by most people.[4]

When too much water is diverted from natural storage locations (whether snowpacks, rivers, or underground aquifers) to places other than where it naturally flows (such as man-made reservoirs, aqueducts, farmlands, golf courses, swimming pools), ecosystems are altered and the well-being of the entire planet is impacted.

Water is considered a sign of life. On Earth, where there is water, life tends to thrive. Where there is no water, the land is dry and barren. And no new water is being produced. Here on present-day Earth, the water that flows from our streams and rivers to the lakes and oceans is the same water that flowed during the time of the dinosaurs.

But now Earth's water is being polluted from both industrial and residential sources. And as the overall population grows, the demand for safe, clean water also grows. Plus, there is greater awareness of water-borne diseases spread through the use of contaminated wash and drinking water. Some eye-opening yet troubling statistics include:

- 18% of the world's population has inadequate water.

- 40% lack sanitation treatment to maintain even minimal health standards.
- 80% of sickness in developing countries is traceable to water-related diseases that we take for granted as being easily preventable.[5]

The 216th General Assembly of the Presbyterian Church (USA) affirms that the "issues of water rights and regulatory takings are exceedingly complex," and that the "spirit of love and justice and the creation of humans in the image of God that give foundation to rights are God-given." The General Assembly's report goes on to state that water rights are "limited by the community's responsibility to promote the common good and to restrain those who seek individual gain at the expense of others and the community as a whole."[6]

Sustainable water reclamation and purification technologies (such as Earth-emulating Living Machines[7]) are presently available to solve these problems, given public awareness of the issues coupled with adequate funding to put them in place. Attaining the goals of providing clean drinking, washing, and general sanitation water to populations in need will require the investment of significant amounts of money.

Another option might be redirection of money currently being invested in other sectors (such as cell phone towers and other high-tech infrastructures).

Climate Change

This complex problem includes:

- increasing average global air and ocean temperatures
- widespread melting of snow and ice
- decreasing average annual Arctic sea ice extent over the last thirty years by 2.7% per decade in winter, and 7.4% per decade in summer
- decreasing mountain glaciers and snow cover in both hemispheres
- rising average global sea levels at an average rate of 1.8 mm/year since 1961
- warming being greatest at higher northern latitudes
- land regions warming faster than oceans
- increasing intense tropical cyclone activity in the North Atlantic since 1970[8]

Many people seem to think that what we hear or read about "climate change" or "global warming" is just a natural variation in Earth's weather patterns. However, evidence shows that humans have enjoyed a long stretch of time (the last twelve thousand years or so) with relatively stable temperatures.

It is important to note that during the last Ice Age (about twenty thousand years ago), when sheets of ice covered the Pacific Northwest, it was only 4°C (about 7°F) cooler. During the twentieth century alone, the average global temperature increase was about 0.6°C, or one full degree Fahrenheit. The rate and duration of warming throughout the twentieth century has been much greater than in any of the previous nine centuries, and the current rate of warming is unprecedented in at least twenty thousand years.[9]

In addition, ice core sample data reveal that the concentration of carbon dioxide in Earth's atmosphere (currently nearly 400 parts per million) is higher now than at any time over at least the past 650,000 years.[10] The vast majority of scientists publishing peer-reviewed climate research today agree that global warming is a man-made phenomenon.[11]

If the Arctic ice continues to melt at close to its current rate, a Northwest Passage along Canada's northern coast could open up permanently within a few short years, which would cut 4,000 nautical miles (7,000 kilometers) off of commercial sea routes between Europe and Asia. Arctic sea traffic would increase suddenly and dramatically. Because the Arctic region contains about 40% of the world's remaining oil and gas reserves, this would open up the area for fossil fuel exploitation. Russia, Denmark, Norway, and Canada, as well as the United States, have already staked claims for resources in that region, and several oil companies have already begun exploratory drilling.[12]

Various impacts projected globally within *this century* include:

- decreased snowpacks
- increased winter floods
- reduced spring/summer melt-related river flows
- heightened competition for over-allocated water resources
- initial increase in aggregate yields of rain-fed agriculture, with variability among regions
- adverse effects on crops already near the warm end of their suitable temperature range or dependent on over-allocated water resources
- heat wave–prone cities being faced with an increased number, intensity, and duration of heat waves

- coastal communities and habitats being increasingly impacted by climate change effects combined with growth, development, and pollution
- an increased spread of diseases[13]

Whether people agree that global warming is anthropogenic (caused by humans) or not, its predicted effects will be hard to ignore. The obvious choice for the best possible collective outcome is to work together to do what we can to prevent and mitigate the worst-case scenarios. Those who adhere to biblical beliefs especially might want to consider their responsibility to lead the way.

Deforestation and Loss of Biodiversity

The issues of deforestation and loss of biodiversity go hand in hand, so we'll look at them together. Various causes of species decline include:

- habitat loss and degradation
- nonnative species being introduced
- overexploitation (overhunting/overfishing)
- disease and parasites

- changing ecological interactions
- climate change

The amount of clear-cut previously forested areas now exceeds the area of remaining rain forest timber stands. This is one of the main causes of biodiversity loss. The issue of harvesting forests in developing countries is quite complex, with obvious economic as well as environmental ramifications.

So What?

With all the difficulties in the world, some might ask why we humans should care about the protection of other species or our environment. The primary secular approaches to this question include

- the Anthropocentric Ethic, which views other species as having utilitarian, aesthetic, educational, and/or spiritual value to humans;
- the Biocentric Ethic, in which all living things have intrinsic value that humans must recognize and respect;
- the Deep Ecology Perspective, which asserts the holistic quality of nature and that our utter dependence on it must be respected; and

- the Eco-Feminism Perspective, which asserts that the nurturing quality of nature must be emphasized and respected.[14]

Professor Max Oehlschlaeger, philosopher at the University of North Texas, wrote that most of Western civilization holds the following position relative to the environment (dubbed Oehlschlaeger's Dominant Western Social Matrix, or ODWSM):

- Nonhuman creation has instrumental or human-oriented value only; claims of biocentric value have no place.
- Short-term economic interests override long-term concerns.
- Environmental risks (including species losses) are acceptable if they are economically beneficial.
- Environmental risks (including species losses) pose no limits to growth, only challenges requiring technological solutions.
- Science and technology will ultimately allow us to maintain essential processes of the biosphere within acceptable limits.

- The politics of interest will be sufficient to ensure the best uses of technology.[15]

ODWSM is a very Machiavellian or results-focused outlook. It's a bit depressing to think that most of the Western world views the environment from such a utilitarian perspective. However, it goes a long way toward explaining why Western cultures have stood by and allowed rampant deforestation and other biodiversity losses to take place, as well as some of the other environmental travesties.

Is the Christian motivation for caring about the earth and the other living things that inhabit it any different from that of the rest of Western civilization? Most thinking, caring Christ followers consider themselves to be stewards of creation. *Stewardship* may be an overused word and/or carry negative associations in today's parlance. But what exactly does it mean? In the best sense of the word, stewardship is management or care that is exercised by one individual on behalf of another.

So, where did this idea of environmental stewardship come from? Caring for creation is a God-given responsibility assigned to the first man and woman and every human being to come after them. "God blessed them: 'Prosper! Reproduce! Fill Earth! Take charge! Be responsible for fish in the sea and birds in the air, for every living thing that moves on the face of Earth'" (Genesis 1:28 MSG).

William Johnson of Arizona State University identified nine environmental themes woven throughout the Old and New Testaments.[16] These include:

1. ***Creation by God***, who called his creation "good":
   * Genesis 1:31—God saw all that he had made, and it was very good.
   * Jeremiah 32:17—Ah Lord GOD! It is thou who hast made the heavens and the earth by thy great power and by thy outstretched arm! Nothing is too hard for thee (RSV).

2. ***Human Stewardship***, in which God gives humans responsibility for creation:
   * Genesis 1:28—God blessed the humans by saying to them, "Be fruitful, multiply, fill the earth, and subdue it! Be masters over the fish in the ocean, the birds that fly, and every living thing that crawls on the earth!" (ISV).

- Deuteronomy 22:6–7—If you chance to come upon a bird's nest, in any tree or on the ground, with young ones or eggs and the mother sitting upon the young or upon the eggs, you shall not take the mother with the young; you shall let the mother go (RSV).
- Hebrews 2:8—You have put all things in subjection under his feet (NASB).

3. *Provision by God* for humankind through creation:
   - Genesis 1:29—And God said, "Behold, I have given you every plant yielding seed which is upon the face of all the earth, and every tree with seed in its fruit; you shall have them for food" (RSV).
   - Ruth 1:6—The LORD had come to the aid of his people by providing food for them.
   - Matthew 5:45—For he makes his sun rise on the evil and on the good, and sends rain on the just and on the unjust (RSV).

4. *Pleasure of God* in his creation:
   - Deuteronomy 11:12—It is a land the LORD your God cares for; the eyes of the LORD your God are continually on it from the beginning of the year to its end.

- John 3:16—For God so loved [his creation] that he gave his only Son, that whoever believes in him should not perish but have eternal life (RSV).

- Revelation 4:11—Worthy, O Master! Yes, our God! Take the glory! the honor! the power! You created it all; it was created because you wanted it (MSG).

5. *Praise*, wherein all of creation praises their Creator:

- Psalm 69:34—You heavens, praise him; praise him, earth; also ocean and all things that swim in it (MSG).

- Revelation 5:13—And I heard every creature in heaven and on earth and under the earth and in the sea, and all therein, saying, "To him who sits upon the throne and to the Lamb be blessing and honor and glory and might for ever and ever!" (RSV).

6. *Authority of God* over his creation:

- 1 Kings 18:1—During the third year without rain, the LORD spoke his word to Elijah: "Go and meet King Ahab, and I will soon send rain" (NCV).

- Luke 8:25—He said to them, "Where is your faith?" And they were afraid, and they marveled, saying to one another, "Who then is this, that he commands even wind and water, and they obey him?" (RSV).

7. ***Witness of Nature*** to God's authority and provision:

    - Exodus 9:29—Moses said, "As soon as I'm out of the city, I'll stretch out my arms to GOD. The thunder will stop and the hail end so you'll know that the land is GOD's land" (MSG).

    - Acts 14:17—Yet he has not left himself without testimony: He has shown kindness by giving you rain from heaven and crops in their seasons; he provides you with plenty of food and fills your hearts with joy.

8. ***Consequences to Creation***—including humans—for mankind's wickedness:

    - Jeremiah 12:4—How long will the land lie parched and the grass in every field be withered? Because those who live in it are wicked, the animals and birds have perished. Moreover, the people are saying, "He will not see what happens to us."

    - Revelation 11:18—The nations were angry; and your wrath has come. The time has come for judging the dead, and for rewarding your servants the prophets and your saints and those who reverence your name, both small and great—and for destroying those who destroy the earth.

9. ***Perspective***—God Most High is above his creation in both position and authority:

- Psalm 113:3–6—From the rising of the sun to the place where it sets, the name of the LORD is to be praised. The LORD is exalted over all the nations, his glory above the heavens. Who is like the LORD our God, the One who sits enthroned on high, who stoops down to look on the heavens and the earth?

- Matthew 12:8, 11–12—"For the Son of Man is Lord of the Sabbath" . . . He said to them, "If any of you has a sheep and it falls into a pit on the Sabbath, will you not take hold of it and lift it out? How much more valuable is a man than a sheep! Therefore it is lawful to do good on the Sabbath."

These nine biblical themes supply a solid foundation for Christians to frame their positions on environmental care. However, many believers only use portions of them in responding to the ecological crisis. Reverend Jim Ball, executive director of the Evangelical Environmental Network, refers to four distinct frameworks (of basic beliefs about the world and our place in it) that various individual believers hold relative to stewardship of God's creation:

- Wise Use
- Anthropocentric Stewardship
- Caring Management
- Servant Stewardship[17]

The Reverend Ball and Dr. Randy Van Dragt from Calvin College give us further insight into each of these frameworks as follows:

Wise Use

In this framework, God is seen as the ultimate Provider of resources for human use, with the goal of maximizing human good. Humans are considered to be the rulers God put over his creation. The rest of creation (ROC) is viewed as providing resources for human use, with human-attributed value only. Humans are to make effective and efficient use of ROC. The emphasis of this framework is stewardship rhetoric that provides a guise for exploitation. The prevailing attitude of those who hold this view is extreme arrogance toward the environment. A scriptural basis for this framework is attributed to a precritical understanding of Genesis chapters 1–11.

Anthropocentric Stewardship

This framework portrays God as the Creator and Owner of creation, with the goal of maximizing human benefit while conserving ROC. Humans are considered to be the kings with power over creation. ROC is viewed as providing resources for human use, but also as God's property. Because God is the Owner of creation, wasteful use of ROC could be considered sinful. Value is attributed to ROC by both God and humans, with humans having the highest value and thus taking priority.

People are to take what they need, but they also should be working to improve ROC. The emphases of this framework are based on the notion that human redemption has implications for ROC, so complying with God's commands and leaving resources for future generations are chief ethical guidelines. However, the prevailing attitude is still arrogance toward ROC. The scriptural basis for this framework is attributed to a precritical understanding of Genesis chapters 1–11, along with Psalm 24 and Matthew 6.

Caring Management

In this framework, God is seen as the Creator and Owner who loves ROC, but loves humans even more. The goal is to have humans and creation flourish and thrive under caring management. Humans are seen as the lords and servants of creation. ROC is viewed as resources and fellow creatures with intrinsic value, however with less than that of human beings. ROC can be sinned against.

People are to make effective and efficient use of ROC. They are to nurture and use ROC sustainably, and plans are to be carefully evaluated vis-à-vis their impacts on ROC. The emphases of this framework are cosmic redemption, the human Imago Dei (being made in the image of God), and responsibility. The prevailing attitude is paternalism toward ROC. The scriptural foundation for this framework is attributed to a more contextual and charitable understanding of Genesis chapters 1 and 2, and the cosmic redemption described in John 3:16.

Servant Stewardship

This framework views God as the Creator and Redeemer of all. As such, he loves and desires *shalom* (peace, well-being, perfection) for all creation with the goal of all creation flourishing. Human beings are seen as servants, keepers, and preservers of ROC. Other species (plant and animal) are viewed as fellow members of Christ's creation, with intrinsic value. As such, ROC can be sinned against. Humans are to live so as to preserve and nurture all of creation. The emphases of this framework are cosmic redemption, with human uniqueness downplayed and Christ's servanthood as the key paradigm.

Human responsibility is stressed over and above human priority, and the prevailing attitude is humility toward the environment. The scriptural foundation for this framework is attributed to a more contextual and charitable understanding of Genesis 1 and 2, Psalm 104, and Philippians 2.[18]

Making It Personal

To determine what position we should take as Christ-followers, we might do well to ask ourselves and each other the following questions:

How do we, or better yet, how ought we to view God relative to creation?

- Is he merely a Provider of resources for human use?
- Or is he Creator, Redeemer, Lover, Sustainer, and Restorer of all creation?

How ought we to see the value and moral status of the rest of creation?

- Does it have value in providing resources for humans only?
- Or does it have God-given value as it includes fellow members of creation, testifying to and glorifying God, worthy of Christ's redemption?

What ought to be the human role relative to the rest of creation?

- Is it merely to be users and exploiters?
- Or is it to be image-bearers of God, servants and lords of creation, caretakers, preservers, and nurturers, even prayer warriors and teachers of others?

What ought to be our attitude toward the rest of creation?

- Condescension and arrogance?
- Or rather, humility, appreciation, contentment, delight, and care?

Perhaps it's easy and tempting to think, *I'm just one person—what difference can I possibly make?* But I'd like to encourage you to believe that one passionate, inspired person can make a difference, and as everyone does their own part, together we'll preserve our planet and its resources for generations to come. Instead of asking hopelessly, "What can I do?" we should really be asking ourselves, "What *should* I do to care for my Father's world?" That is our ethical dilemma.

We also might consider Professor Max Oelschlaeger's challenge to the church:

> I think of religion, or more specifically the church . . . as being more important in the effort to conserve life on earth than all the politicians and experts put together. The church may be, in fact, our last, best chance. My conjecture is this: There are no solutions for the systemic causes of ecocrisis, at least in democratic societies, apart from religious narrative.[19]

Keeping that challenge in mind, we can study, contemplate, and discuss with humility what ought to be our proper perspective on God, ourselves, and the rest of creation, as well as the values and interrelationships of all these entities. Then, after framing our perspective, the next vital step is to discover what actions are required to best put into practice our environmental code of ethics.

It's Up to Us

God ordained the natural physical laws to provide order in the universe. Perhaps at least part of the reason he did that was to allow humans to practice free will.

Our rational, orderly universe provides a place wherein actions have predictable consequences. As a result of the consistent and reliable laws of physics, cause and effect are closely coupled. When we choose a particular course of action, we can fairly well foresee the direct and immediate effects and consequences of that action.

Keeping this in mind, imagine that a guy with a gun walks into a crowded arena and starts shooting. He knows in advance that his freely chosen willful action will cause pain, suffering, and quite possibly death to others.

If God intervened by violating the laws of physics to prevent bad consequences from ever happening, then our orderly world would become chaotic and capricious—cause and effect would be decoupled and actions would have no predictable consequences. Free will would essentially become meaningless.

The problem of evil is the age-old stumbling block to faith in God. Perhaps free will is such an important part of what it means to be human that evil is an unavoidable consequence.

Apparently it was important enough to God that he would let his own Son die for the possibility that we would choose to believe.

And, considering all the Creator did for us, it seems imperative that we use our free will to take care of this world. There isn't any other. Or, is there?

9 The Universe: Are We Alone?

O N THE DARKEST, clearest night, from Earth we can see only a couple thousand stars with the naked eye, yet powerful ground-and space-based telescopes have revealed billions. The vastness of the universe is impossible for most people to comprehend.

Though the observable universe is thought to be about ninety billion light-years across, scientists don't really know how large the entire universe is. Most of it can't be seen. Yet Psalm 147:4 tells us that God "counts the number of the stars; He gives names to all of them" (NASB).

Have you ever wondered whether there's anyone else out there?

If our universe is so huge, maybe other intelligent beings are out there somewhere. Researchers for the Search for Extra-Terrestrial Intelligence (SETI) program have been analyzing radio signals from space using various telescopes since 1978. In close to four decades they have not yet detected anything that could be construed as a signal from an intelligent civilization. Since radio waves travel at the speed of light, this means we're pretty sure there are no other technological civilizations within about forty light-years from Earth—otherwise we'd have heard something by now.

Exploring the Final Frontier

Still, our search for extrasolar planets, or exoplanets (planets orbiting other stars), continues. So far thousands have been detected, and over 40% of those have been confirmed. It's hard to find them because they are so far away, and they're very dim compared to the stars they orbit. This makes direct observation and imaging of these planets pretty rare.

But there are several other ways to detect them. The first is by the slight gravitational tug on their star as they orbit it, causing the star to wobble a bit. Astronomers can detect this wobble in two ways: (1) through astrometry, which precisely measures the position of the star over time, and (2) by periodic changes in the star's light. Starlight is blue-shifted to shorter wavelengths when the planet tugs the star toward us on the near side of the star. It's red-shifted to longer wavelengths when the planet tugs the star away from us on the far side of the star. This Doppler effect is analogous to the shift in the frequency of sound waves to a higher pitch (shorter wavelengths) when a siren is coming toward us and a lower pitch (longer wavelengths) when the siren moves away.

Another way to detect extrasolar planets is by the small drop in starlight when a planet crosses directly in front of its star. This transit photometry method is very difficult to accomplish because the plane of the planet's orbit has to be directly in line with our viewing angle here on Earth.

Other detection methods include polarimetry (polarization of starlight by the atmosphere of an exoplanet), gravitational microlensing (exoplanets' contribution to the lensing effect of their star), timing variations (changes in periodic phenomena, such as pulsars), and orbital brightness modulations (changes in the star's apparent brightness due to the planet moving around it, e.g., planetary phases).

Even though as many as 20% of sun-like stars in the universe might have an Earth-sized planet in their circumstellar habitable zones (not too close/hot; not too far/cold)—and with the help of NASA's Kepler Mission thousands of extra-solar planets have already been detected—exploration efforts so far have not revealed any other places in the universe quite like Earth. Most of the exoplanets detected so far are big like Jupiter, and orbit fairly close to their stars, but this is probably mostly because it is easier to detect these types of planets. Still, as discussed in chapter 7, it's clear that a lot of things have to go just right to produce all the conditions necessary to support life on any planet.

Yet every year thousands of people report unidentified flying object (UFO) sightings. Fully one-half of all Americans believe in extraterrestrial life. In fact, 47% of Americans believe that UFOs are evidence of aliens. However, 95% of the reported UFO sightings are accounted for as man-made objects or natural phenomenon, with most of them fitting into one of these four categories:

1. hoaxes (typically devised by clever young adults with too much time on their hands)
2. overly active imaginations
3. misidentification of natural phenomenon
4. misidentification of unknown technology

Some of the main examples are fireballs (which are meteors that come close to the observer). These can appear to be up to four times the size of the moon. Or Venus in the morning, which appears very large and bright. Other common examples are weather balloons, atmospheric effects (such as swamp gas or northern and southern lights), military aircraft (such as various stealth technologies), or hydrogen balloons exploding. The remaining roughly 5% seem to be inexplicable.

Defying Explanation

So, let's spend a little time talking about the inexplicable 5%. I'm especially grateful to my friends Dr. Hugh Ross and professor Kenneth Samples at Reasons to Believe for sharing their research on this topic in their book, *Lights in the Sky and Little Green Men*.[1]

These inexplicable UFOs seem to defy the laws of physics. They appear capable of making impossibly abrupt 90° movements at tens of thousands of miles per hour, disintegrating, then reappearing and changing forms. Sometimes they appear to leave physical effects without any apparent physical cause, such as "crop circles," burnt or bent grass without crash debris, radio interference, and malfunctioning electrical systems.

For these sightings to be taken seriously, there must be at least two credible eyewitnesses. In addition, some reports indicate that animals (such as cows and dogs) have also been affected by or exhibited strange behavior after such sightings. That makes it even more difficult to write off inexplicable UFO sightings as merely psychological phenomenon.

So, what are the options for these inexplicable UFOs? Of the alternatives, three are most frequently proposed:

1. misidentified natural or physical phenomena
2. actual extraterrestrials sending UFOs to Earth
3. extradimensional beings (which are real but nonphysical entities that can transcend space and time)

Most of the time, the first option can be rejected right away because the inexplicable objects violate the laws of physics. That means they can't rationally be explained as physical, natural objects. Even if some mistakenly labeled inexplicable UFOs might fall into this category, it certainly can't explain *most* of them.

Numerous Complications

So, could it be possible that intelligent extraterrestrial beings are sending UFOs to Earth? As discussed in chapter 7, the number of conditions necessary for life in any particular star-planet system, combined with the amount of time and complex processes involved in producing intelligent life, as well as the limited time frame that a planet remains habitable, make it extremely unlikely to find another planet in the universe capable of sustaining intelligent life. Especially during the same time frame that life exists on Earth. In fact, by some estimations, a person is more likely to win the California state lottery more than five thousand times in a row than we are apt to discover another life-friendly planet.

In addition, there are several problems with the idea that UFOs might be coming from distant planets.

The Distance Problem

SETI recently estimated that there are no extrasolar planets suitable for life within at least 155 light-years from Earth. To get a better sense of what scientists have discovered so far in our galactic neighborhood, a list of the closest neighboring stars and significant extrasolar planets includes:

- Alpha Centauri triple star: 4.3 light-years (LY) from Earth; possible unconfirmed exoplanet;
- Tau Ceti e: 11.9 LY from Earth; closest unconfirmed terrestrial-class planet in habitable zone (4.3 Earth masses); might be capable of supporting primitive thermophilic life;
- Gliese 674 b: 14.8 LY from Earth; closest confirmed exoplanet (11 Earth masses); orbits very close to its star;
- 82 G Eridani c: 20 LY from Earth; the smallest confirmed exoplanet (2.4 Earth masses) within 50 light-years of Earth;
- Gliese 581: 20.4 LY from Earth; system of relatively low-mass exoplanets within a star's habitable zone;
- Kepler 186 f: 500 LY from Earth; first Earth-sized planet (~1.1 times Earth's radius) orbiting in its star's habitable zone.

Then there is the closely related *velocity* problem. With our current spacecraft and rocket technology, we can travel only a little faster than one-thousandth (1/1000th) of the speed of light (for space-nerds like me, that's 0.0014c or 0.14% of the speed of light), so we're talking about it taking thousands or even hundreds of thousands of years to travel to or from any of these other places.

The Time and Weight Problems

At 0.14% of the speed of light, it would take 3,071 years to get to the next closest star system of Alpha Centauri; 8,500 years to get to Tau Ceti e; 10,571 years to get to Gliese 674 b; 14,285 years to get to 82 G Eridani c; 14,571 years to get to Gliese 581; 110,714 years to get to the frontier of the closest possible SETI-estimated habitable planet; and 357,143 years to get to the recently discovered Kepler 186 f. Just try to imagine the implications of these spaceflight durations in terms of being able to come in contact with other possible intelligent life!

Next, there's the *weight* problem. Any interstellar spacecraft and its crew would need protection from radiation and meteoroid impacts, and the faster they go, the worse the potential impact problem becomes, because energy (and thus damage) increases with the square of velocity. So, if they go two times faster, the damage from a meteoroid impact increases by a factor of four; three times faster, and the damage increases by a factor of nine; and so on.

Therefore, the faster they go, the more protection they need. That would add to the spacecraft's weight, which makes it more difficult to go fast, so it's really a vicious cycle of increasing speed, shielding, and weight. Even if propulsion technology made significant advances, it is commonly thought that anything with mass of any size could only ever travel at a maximum speed of one-tenth of the speed of light (0.1c), so even if you could go nearly a hundred times faster, it would still take at least 1,550 years to travel SETI's projected minimum distance.

The Numbers Problem and Wormholes

Any other civilization would have to send out about ten thousand spacecraft per year to account for the number of sightings. And, so many different UFO designs have been reported that this would be a ridiculous proposition.

Even if humans aren't yet capable of traveling the long interstellar distances between Earth and other possible habitable planets, is it possible that other intelligent extraterrestrial beings are? People always ask the obvious question: "What if these ETs have technology that is way ahead of ours?" Dr. Michio Kaku from City College of New York conveyed these relevant thoughts:

Alien intelligence will have to conform to the laws of physics as we know them. However, there are loopholes [for example, wormholes] in the laws of physics that have to be investigated . . . This wormhole allows you to leap across vast distances within the twinkling of an eye without violating Einstein's theory of general relativity . . . However . . . we still don't know whether or not the wormhole is stable once we take into account radiation effects . . . We don't know what lies on the other side of the wormhole.[2]

It is quite unlikely that anyone would ever find what is required for a wormhole existing in real physical space. There would need to be two black holes joined together back to back. However, the mathematical calculations based on relativity theory all seem to indicate that if the Planck energy (10^{19} billion electron volts) could be harnessed, then a hole could open up in space and time. Yet even if this did occur, the wormhole would be highly unstable and wouldn't last very long. Furthermore, nothing larger than a subatomic particle would be likely to survive the intense gravitational stretching (or "spaghettification") that is thought to occur in passing through a wormhole.

Space-Travel Problems

Suppose for a moment that there is extraterrestrial life somewhere out there. After all, one might say since it happened here on Earth, perhaps it might have happened under the same conditions and/or for the same reasons (purposeful or otherwise) somewhere else. Let's talk a little about the problems for living, intelligent creatures to travel long distances in space to come to Earth. If the only life possible is life as we know it, then reason and logic tell us that the problems humans have would be similar to problems that other complex, intelligent beings would have.

The unique environmental conditions of spaceflight produce a variety of mostly negative physiological and psychological effects in humans that include:

- space adaptation syndrome, which is motion sickness in space
- severe cardiovascular deconditioning
- progressive osteoporosis

- immune system suppression
- radiation-related cellular damage and mutations
- psychological problems

As a result of these issues and the great expense and mass associated with keeping humans (or even animals) alive in space, NASA has figured out that the farther away we want to explore, the more economical it is to send machines instead of living beings. Besides with all of these negative effects, why would anyone willingly choose to take that risk? A variety of answers have been given to this age-old question, such as human curiosity, the spirit of adventure, exploring the frontier, pushing the envelope of human capabilities, ensuring the future of human civilization, or simply "because it's there!" After recently being asked to consider going on a possible round-trip planetary flyby mission, my adventurous side quickly overruled all of the risks involved. Subsequently that opportunity was put on hold, but if it reemerges, I'd still be up for it.

Still, some of my student researchers have been working with me on addressing the issues associated with keeping humans healthy as they travel in space. One of these projects involved the design of a life-support system for a long-duration mission to the moon. In studying what it takes to support human life if we travel anywhere else in the universe, my students have been learning to appreciate how special our planet is.

Questions Remain

In spite of all the real-world physical problems, some people still insist that there's a government conspiracy to cover up what is actually known about UFOs. Unanswered questions persist about things that have taken on an almost legendary status, such as the Roswell incident, Project Blue Book, and the US Air Force's Area 51 in Nevada.

On June 14, 1947, something crashed to the ground in Roswell, New Mexico. A spokesperson for the US Air Force (USAF) announced that the roughly 5 pounds of crash site debris was the wreckage of a high-altitude weather balloon. In the 1990s, the Air Force reported that the Roswell debris was from a top-secret high-altitude balloon associated with Project Mogul, designed to acoustically detect Soviet nuclear detonations and ballistic missiles.

The USAF's Project Blue Book started in the early 1950s, during the McCarthy Era. The thinking behind this research and cataloguing project was that the USSR might use bogus

UFOs to cause hysteria or that UFO sightings might clog communications channels. Dr. Mark Clark, director of national security studies at Cal State, San Bernardino, wrote, "There is a government 'conspiracy' to keep security issues secret from other countries or enemies who could use it against us."[3] In other words, the government does hide information for security purposes. High-tech military technology fits into this classification.

During the time frame of the mid- to late-1950s, fully half of the UFO sightings were U2 spy plane sightings. The U2 flies at very high altitudes, and because its exterior was originally unpainted aluminum, it reflected sunlight after sunset so it looked like a bright and fast-moving object. Many advanced aircraft on so-called black budget projects (programs that don't show up in the public versions of the federal budget), such as U2s, SR-71 Blackbirds, the Stealth Bomber, Stealth Fighter, and Unmanned Aerial Vehicles, were developed or tested in Area 51. That's a military site covering about 4,600 square miles, which sits near the dry bed of Groom Lake, roughly eighty miles northwest of Las Vegas.

In spite of all the rumors and sci-fi TV shows and movies, very few serious UFO researchers actually believe that alien beings have been recovered, dead or alive. A UFO or alien conspiracy would be very difficult to keep completely under wraps for nearly seven decades, because so many people would have had to keep quiet for such a long time, even when lured by the possibility of making big money from telling their stories.

The Watergate Era spawned a generation of government mistrust and conspiracy theorists. But the fact that the missing eighteen or so minutes on the infamous Nixon tapes remained covered up for only days makes a conspiracy theory all the more implausible.

Another Possibility

The third and final option for the remaining inexplicable 5% of UFO sightings focuses on the possibility of extradimensional entities not bound by our physical dimensions of space and time. A few well-documented accounts of alien abductions include events from:

- September 1961: A couple driving through the mountains in New Hampshire sees a large pancake-shaped craft flying toward them. Later, they can't account for two missing hours; they experienced various ongoing physical problems and nightmares suggesting repressed memories of alien abduction.

- November 1975: Six men reported that a colleague disappeared when he approached a UFO; five days later he showed up, mentally disturbed and dehydrated, reporting that he had been examined by aliens.

Previously it was mentioned that UFO sightings consistently show them appearing to defy the laws of physics, making sharp 90° turns at tens of thousands of miles per hour, changing form, and disintegrating then reappearing. If these UFOs were not physical, then they wouldn't be bound by the laws of physics. But what would it mean to say that they are both real and nonphysical?

Everything real is not necessarily physical. UFO researcher Dr. Jacques Vallee agrees that "the UFO phenomenon" represents evidence for other dimensions beyond space and time.[4] General relativity and Big Bang cosmology both indicate that the cause of the universe is beyond physical space and time.

The reliability and credibility of the Bible (discussed in chapters 4 and 5) provide confidence in what the Bible says about nonphysical reality. The Bible is the only holy book that refers to a God who transcends space and time. Furthermore, Scripture speaks of nonphysical extradimensional entities, whether good or evil. They, too, are capable of transcending space and time.

We've all seen or at least heard of the classic 1977 movie, *Close Encounters of the Third Kind*. The following list defines the various levels of encounters:

1st kind: close visual sightings
2nd kind: physical effects on the environment
3rd kind: contact with an alien or a being from a UFO
4th kind: abduction by alien beings
5th kind: permanent physical harm or death

Some common threads shared among UFO experiences seem to correlate more strongly with the higher levels of close encounters. First, eyewitnesses are often involved in occult practices, such as seeking supernatural knowledge, predicting the future with tarot cards, astrology, witchcraft, séances, channeling spirits, poltergeist phenomena, levitation, serious or black magic; even things as seemingly innocuous as Ouija boards.

Second, deception is typically involved about the nature of the UFO or alien, about communicating the motivation, intent, or ideas, and even deception or inaccuracies about science and technology.

Third, malevolence or harm to the eyewitnesses is prevalent on various levels, such as mental, emotional, physical, and psychological, sometimes getting progressively worse as time passes. People are taken against their will, and crude examinations or operations are performed.

Fourth, peak sightings are typically in the middle of the night, along remote lonely roads. Counter to what would be expected if these were actually physical objects, mainstream professional astronomers (who, at over a thousand hours per year, are observing more than most anyone else) are not the ones reporting UFO encounters.

And fifth, UFO scientific knowledge roughly keeps pace with popular science fiction, slightly beyond what the average layperson would know, but slightly behind what cutting-edge research is discovering. These UFO entities don't seem to be on top of the accurate and current state-of-the-art science and technology. For example, speeds of these craft have increased from quite slow in the days of blimps to closer to those of modern-day spacecraft. Also, in the earliest reports, aliens claimed to be from the moon, then from Venus, then from Mars, and now from other star systems—keeping pace with human discoveries that each of these former places were uninhabitable. If supposed aliens were technologically and scientifically advanced, we could expect them to be scientifically accurate.

The Reality

From this perspective, it seems implausible. These beings are *not* smarter than us, highly sophisticated, or benevolent, as one might expect highly advanced civilizations to be. None of this fits well with the type of scientific and technological sophistication necessary for intelligent extraterrestrials to be successfully sending physical spacecraft across the vast reaches of space.

By analysis and the process of elimination, the third option for the remaining inexplicable 5% of UFO sightings fits the evidence better than any of the other options. Some people who think they have seen a UFO, but who are not involved in the occult, may have seen an IFO (an identifiable flying object), or may not realize they've opened themselves up to occult influences. The number and frequency of UFO sightings are higher in countries where occult involvement is higher.

And UFO messengers are reported as encouraging belief in the practices of channeling, reincarnation, and mysticism.

In evaluating the existence of UFOs, we can eliminate the first categorical option of misidentified natural physical objects, because apart from some mistakes in classification, inexplicable UFOs violate the laws of physics. With respect to the second option, from a purely naturalistic viewpoint, the probabilities examined within the context of the Anthropic or Goldilocks Principle (see chapter 7) would tell us that it's unlikely for life to even be here on Earth, let alone anywhere else in the universe.

From a Christian perspective, there is nothing in Scripture that says God has not created life elsewhere in the universe. On the other hand, current scientific knowledge, as well as empirical evidence, weighs heavily against any extraterrestrial civilizations ever being able to reach us due to the problems of distance, velocity, time, weight, numbers, wormholes, and physiology. On his website, Christian apologist Carmen DiCello wrote:

> If inter-dimensional beings really do exist, this would explain their presence among us, without having to deal with the massive

distances that extraterrestrials would need to travel. On top of this, scientists have already shown that other dimensions probably do exist . . . This doesn't prove that UFOs are interdimensional, but it certainly allows for the possibility. Furthermore, the spiritual/religious aspects of this phenomenon seem to demand a spiritual explanation. This doesn't necessitate that we reject other viable alternatives. Neither does our explanation of these matters need to be simplistic and singular; in fact, a complex explanation of the phenomenon is probable. From a biblical perspective, however, it is difficult to ignore the reality that some portion (perhaps the majority) of this puzzling array of seemingly paranormal activity demands an inter-dimensional . . . interpretation.[5]

All that said, the Bible and science taken together can inform our perspective. Especially when we are willing to remain open to new evidence and repeat the steps of the scientific method—collecting observational data, then forming and testing our best hypotheses to refine our explanations. For now, the third categorical option seems to fit best with the evidence—extradimensional nonphysical realities bound neither by space and time, nor by physical laws, are most consistent with the common threads of UFO encounters and correlate with worldwide levels of occult involvement.

Conclusion

Our Future with Science and Faith

MY QUESTIONS ABOUT science and faith started with trying to reconcile my experiences at church with my experiences in the classroom. They were a big part of my search for meaning and purpose. Fortunately, through persistent study, I've been able to find satisfying answers to the questions that continually come up—questions like: Who is God? What's his character like? Does he care about humanity? Has he made other realms? How does nature fit with the Bible? Can a person be a Christian and a scientist?

To ensure that talented people of faith continue contributing to the sciences, we need to show young people that they don't have to choose between science and faith. Being both a good scientist and a faithful Christian is possible, and though I'm certainly not perfect, I am living proof that the two disciplines can be reconciled to provide a fascinating life filled with purpose and meaning.

Along the way I've discovered some helpful tips for getting more comfortable with the science and faith dialogue. We can:

1. Approach this dialogue with humility and grace, for "now we see through a glass, darkly" (1 Corinthians 13:12 KJV).

2. Try to understand the spectrum of positions and arguments on all sides.

3. Realize that most people are on a journey, still figuring out where they stand.

4. Recognize that these issues are not fundamental to your faith or your salvation.

5. Learn to live with the tension. It's alright *not* to have it all figured out or to have all the "right" answers.

6. Keep arguments or disagreements from upsetting us. We need to remember that if we could prove God's existence in an open-and-shut case, we'd have no need of faith.

7. Heed Saint Augustine's wise advice: "In essentials, unity; in non-essentials, liberty; in all things, charity."[1]

The cycle of new scientific discoveries, followed by adjustments in our interpretation of Scripture relative to our understanding of God's interaction with the physical world, continues to repeat itself. Keeping that in mind can prepare us to avoid a crisis of faith if or when we discover convincing evidence for a multiverse, or intelligent life on a newly discovered exoplanet. We know God is good. We know he loves us. We know he provides lavishly for us. By taking him out of the box of our finite understanding, we can worship him as he truly is: sometimes not safe, but always good.

Notes

Chapter 1

1. Saint Augustine (AD 354–430) in his work *The Literal Meaning of Genesis* (De Genesi ad litteram libri duodecim); this translation is by J. H. Taylor in *Ancient Christian Writers* (Mahwah, NJ: Paulist Press, 1982), volume 41.

2. Since then attributed to galactic dust; Rown Cowen and *Nature* magazine, "Gravitational Waves Discovery Now Officially Dead: Data from the South Pole experiment BICEP2 and the Planck probe point to galactic dust as a confounding signal" (February 2, 2015), as read in *Scientific American*, www.scientificamerican.com.

3. Leslie Wickman, "Does the Big Bang breakthrough offer proof of God?" available from religion.blogs.cnn.com, accessed 1/26/15.

Chapter 2

1. James Sinclair, "The *Kalam* Cosmological Argument." In *The Blackwell Companion to Natural Theology*, Wm. L. Craig and J. P. Moreland, eds. (Oxford: Wiley-Blackwell, 2009), 101–201.

2. C. S. Lewis, *Mere Christianity* (New York: MacMillan Publishing Co., Inc., 1979), 17–18.

Chapter 3

1. Lord Francis Bacon, *Novum Organum*, edited by Joseph Devey, Forgotten Books (New York: P. F. Collier and Son, 1901), Preface, 6.

2. Melville Y. Stewart, *Science and Religion in Dialog* (West Sussex, UK: Wiley-Blackwell, 2010), 261.

3. Morris Kline, *Mathematics and the Search for Knowledge* (New York: Oxford University Press, 1985), 242.

4. Steven D. Schafersman, *An Introduction to Science: Scientific Thinking and the Scientific Method* (1994), available from geo.sunysb.edu, accessed on 6/27/13.

5. Charles Darwin, *The Variation of Animals and Plants Under Domestication*, Vol. I, (Baltimore: Johns Hopkins University Press, 1998), 25.

6. Jeffrey Nichols, *Scientific Method* (2003), available from naturaltheology.net, accessed 12/9/03.

7. Minucius Felix, *Faith of the Early Fathers: Volume I, Pre-Nicene and Nicene Eras*, W. A. Jurgens, ed. (Collegeville, MN: The Order of St. Benedict, 1970), 109.

8. Bacon, *Novum Organum*, Book 1, Aphorism 129, 105.

9. Michael A. Covington, *Christianity and Science, 1: Scientific Method* (1999); available from covingtoninnovations.com, accessed 6/27/13.

Chapter 4

1. Raimon Panikkar. *The Intra-Religious Dialog* (Mahwah, NJ: Paulist Press, 1999), 5.

2. David Smith, *B. B. Warfield's Scientifically Constructive Theological Scholarship* (Eugene, OR: Pickwick Publications, 2011), 230.

3. C. S. Lewis, *Christian Reflections* (Grand Rapids, MI: Wm. B. Eerdmans Publishing Co., 2014), 51.

4. Fritz Schaefer III, "Stephen Hawking, the Big Bang, and God," available from globalwebpost.com/farooqm/study_res/ hawking/schaefer.html, accessed 1/29/15.

5. Lee Strobel, *The Case for a Creator* (Grand Rapids, MI: Zondervan, 2004), 71–72.

6. Stephen Hawking and Roger Penrose, *The Nature of Space and Time,* The Isaac Newton Institute Series of Lectures (Princeton, NJ: Princeton University Press, 1996), 20.

7. Stephen Hawking, *A Brief History of Time* (New York: Bantam, 1988), 122.

8. George Smoot and Keay Davidson, *Wrinkles in Time* (New York: William Morrow and Company, 1993), 135.

9. Roger Penrose. *The emperor's new mind: concerning computers, minds, and the laws of physics* (New York: Oxford University Press, 1989).

10. Fred Hoyle, "The Universe: Past and Present Reflections," *Engineering and Science*, November 1981, 8–12.

11. Paul Little, *Know Why You Believe* (Downers Grove, IL: InterVarsity Press, 2008), 99.

12. Nelson Glueck, *Rivers in the Desert* (New York: Farrar, Strous, and Cudahy, 1959), 136.

13. W. F. Albright, *The Archaeology of Palestine*, 1954 edition, quoted in Walter F. Kaiser, "What Good Is Biblical Archaeology to Bible Readers?" *Contact*, Winter 05/06, 128, available from gctuedu.com.

14. C. S. Lewis, *C. S. Lewis, Miracles* (San Francisco: Harper, 2001), 5.

15. Jeff Greenberg, "The Worldwide Mission of GeoScience," lecture at Azusa Pacific University, Azusa, CA, 17 October 2007.

16. Little, *Know Why You Believe*, 131.

17. Lee Strobel, *The Case for Faith* (Grand Rapids, MI: Zondervan, 2000), 84.

Chapter 5

1. Josh McDowell, *Evidence That Demands a Verdict* (San Bernardino, CA: Here's Life Publishers, 1979), 65.

2. Ibid., 62.

3. Sir William Ramsay, *The Bearing of Recent Discovery on the Trustworthiness of the New Testament* (London: Hodder and Stoughton, 1915), 222.

4. McDowell, *Evidence That Demands a Verdict*, 45.

5. J. Komoszewski, ed., and Daniel J. Wallace, *Reinventing Jesus: What* The Da Vinci Code *and Other Novel Speculations Don't Tell You* (Grand Rapids, MI: Kregel, 2006), 70.

6. Frederick F. Bruce, *The New Testament Documents: Are They Reliable?* (Grand Rapids, MI: Eerdmans/IVP, 1981), 10.

7. My thoughts were influenced by Scripture, as well as many additional books and websites, including the

following: *A Portrait of Jesus*, Joseph Girzone; *Handbook of Christian Apologetics*, Peter Kreeft and Ronald Tacelli; *Know Why You Believe*, Paul E. Little; *Without a Doubt: Answering the 20 Toughest Faith Questions*, Kenneth Richard Samples; *Who Is Jesus?* Ray Stedman; *Faith and Reason: Why Christianity Makes Sense*, Austin Schmidt and Joseph Perkins; *The Deity of Christ*, Mark Ritter; swordandspirit.com; *The Case for Christ*, Lee Strobel; *Mere Christianity*, C. S. Lewis.

8. Paul Little, *Know Why You Believe* (Downers Grove, IL: InterVarsity Press, 2008), 48–49.

9. C. S. Lewis, *God in the Dock: Essays on Theology and Ethics* (Grand Rapids, MI: Eerdmans, 1970), 66–67.

10. C. S. Lewis, *Mere Christianity* (New York: MacMillan Publishing Co., Inc., 1979), 55–56.

Chapter 6

1. My friend and fellow science and religion scholar Dr. Denis Lamoureux (author of *I Love Jesus and I Accept Evolution* [Eugene, OR: Wipf & Stock, 2009]) generously shared his perspectives with me in this discussion.

2. Gerald Schroeder, *Genesis and the Big Bang* (New York: Bantam, 1992), 16.

3. Max Planck, available from crestroyertheory.com, accessed 1/29/15.

4. Fritz Schaefer III, "Stephen Hawking, the Big Bang, and God," available from globalwebpost.com/farooqm/study_res/ hawking/schaefer.html, accessed on 1/29/15.

5. Albert Einstein, available from simpletoremember.com/ articles/a/einstein/, accessed 1/29/15.

6. John Lennox, *God's Undertaker: Did Science Bury God?* (Oxford: Wilkinson House, 2009), 87.

7. Henry Morris, *The Troubled Waters of Evolution* (San Diego: Creation-Life Publishers, Institute for Creation Research, 1974).

8. Ed Larson and Larry Witham, "Scientists Are Still Keeping the Faith," *Nature,* 3 April 1997, 435–436.

9. Pope John Paul II, "Cosmology and Fundamental Physics," 3 October 1981 to the Pontifical Academy of Sciences, available from ewtn.com, accessed 1/29/15.

10. Pope Francis, "Plenary Address: Evolving Concepts of Nature," 27 October 2014 to the Pontifical Academy of Sciences, available from w2.vatican.va, accessed 1/29/15.

11. Mark Whorton and Hill Roberts, *Holman QuickSource Guide to Understanding Creation*, (Nashville, TN: B&H Publishing Group, 2008), 81.

12. *The New Interpreter's Study Bible—New Revised Standard Version with the Apocrypha*, Romans 1:20; Psalm 19:1–2 (Nashville, TN: Abingdon Press, 2011), 768, 2003.

13. Guido de Bres. *The Belgic Confession* (1561, revised 1619). Available from urclearning.org/2006/07/03/the-belgic-confession/, accessed 1/27/15.

14. Michael Macrone, *Eureka! What Archimedes Really Meant and 80 Other Key Ideas Explained* (New York: Cader Company, Inc., 1994), 82–83.

15. Adapted from Francis Bacon, *The Advancement of Learning*, 1605. Available from archive.org/stream/advancementoflea00baco/, accessed 1/29/15.

Chapter 7

1. Frederic Burnham, in David Briggs, "Science, Religion, Are Discovering Commonality in Big Bang Theory," *Los Angeles Times*, B6–B7, 2 May 1992.

2. William Lane Craig, *Reasonable Faith*, rev. ed. (Wheaton, IL: Crossway, 1994), 83–88.

3. Ron Cottrell, *The Remarkable Spaceship Earth* (Denver, CO: Accent Books, 1982).

4. Mark Ritter, astronomer, teacher, science apologetics website creator. Personal communications, 2002–2014.

5. Fred Hoyle and Chandra Wickramasinghe. *Evolution from Space: A Theory of Cosmic Creationism* (New York: Simon & Schuster, Inc., 1982).

6. Charles B. Thaxton, Walter L. Bradley, Roger L. Olsen, and Dean H. Kenyon, *The Mystery of Life's Origin: Reassessing Current Theories* (New York: Philosophical Library, 1984).

7. William Paley, *The Works of William Paley* (London: A. Chalmers, 1819), 37.

8. Martin E. Marty, *A Short History of Christianity*, 2nd ed. (Philadelphia: Fortress Press, 1987), 245–246.

9. J. D. Barrow and F. J. Tipler, *The Anthropic Cosmological Principle* (New York: Oxford University Press, 1986).

10. Paul Davies, "The Universe—What's the Point?" *Spiritual Information*, Charles L. Harper Jr., ed. (West Conshohocken, PA: Templeton Foundation Press, 2005), 132–135.

11. Lee Strobel, *The Case for Faith* (Grand Rapids, MI: Zondervan, 2000), 129–156.

12. Davies, "The Universe—What's the Point?" 134.

13. Randy Van Dragt and James A. Clark, "Environmental Stewardship: What Are the Roles for Science and Faith?" *Not Just Science*, Dorothy F. Chappell and E. David Cook, eds. (Grand Rapids, MI: Zondervan Publishing House, 2005), 158–171.

14. William H. Lazareth, "We Believe in God the Father," in *Nicene Creation*, Spring 2007. No longer available from carthage.edu, (last accessed 4/21/07), but also in *Confessing the One Faith: An Ecumenical Explication of the Apostolic Faith* (Eugene, OR: Wipf & Stock, 2010), 22.

15. Isaac Newton, *Opticks* (1650), available from goodreads.com/author/quotes/135106.Isaac_Newton, accessed 1/29/15.

16. Lydia Jaeger, "Cosmic Order and Divine Word," in *Spiritual Information*, Charles L. Harper Jr., ed. (West Conshohocken, PA: Templeton Foundation Press, 2005), 151–152.

17. Fred Hoyle (1915–2001). Available from thinkexist.com, accessed 2/2/2015.

18. Antony Flew and Gary R. Habermas, "My Pilgrimage from Atheism to Theism: An Exclusive Interview with Former British Atheist Professor Antony Flew," *Philosophia Christi: Journal of the Evangelical Philosophical Society*, Winter 2005.

19. Paul E. Little, *Know Why You Believe*, 4th ed. (Downers Grove, IL: InterVarsity Press, 2000), ch. 2.

Chapter 8

1. Randy VanDragt and James Clark, "Environmental Stewardship: What are the Roles for Science and Faith?" *Not Just Science* (Grand Rapids, MI: Zondervan, 2005), 158–171.

2. "Daily Temperature Cycle Discussion," available from dailytemperaturecycle.com/, accessed 12/4/08; "World Energy Resources and Consumption," available from wikipedia.org/, accessed 12/4/08.

3. Available from the Climate Project, climateproject.org/, accessed 12/4/08.

4. Peter Gleick, "Water resources," *Encyclopedia of Climate and Weather*, vol. 2, S. H. Schneider, ed. (New York: Oxford University Press, 1996), 817–823.

5. United Nations Department of Economic and Social Affairs, Division for Sustainable Development, *Sustainable Development in the 21st Century: Review of implementation of Agenda 21 and the Rio Principles-DRAFT* (2012), available from un.org/esa/dsd/dsd_sd21st/21_pdf/ SD21_Study1_Agenda21.pdf, accessed 1/29/15.

6. The Advisory Committee on Social Witness Policy of the General Assembly Council, *Limited Water Resources and Takings with Study Guide* (Louisville, KY: Presbyterian Church [USA], 2004), 1–29.

7. Leslie Wickman, "Water Reclamation for Remote Environments: An Ecologically Sound Approach," paper presented/published for 45th American Institute of Aeronautics and Astronautics (AIAA) Aerospace Sciences Meeting (Reno, NV: 2007), 1–8.

8. "Summary for Policymakers of the Synthesis Report of the IPCC (Intergovernmental Panel on Climate Change) Fourth Assessment Report" (Valencia, Spain: IPCC Plenary XXVII, 2007), 1–23.

9. Patrick Smith, *Pathfinder Study: Impact of Global Warming on Space Programs* (El Segundo, CA: The Aerospace Corporation, 2007), 1–45.

10. "New evidence extends greenhouse gas record from ice cores by 50 percent, adding 210,000 years," American Association for the Advancement of Science news release, 24 November 2005.

11. T. F. Stocker, D. Qin, G. K. Plattner, M. Tignor, S. K. Allen, J. Boschung, A. Nauels, Y. Xia, V. Bex, and P. M. Midgley, eds., "IPCC, 2013: Summary for Policymakers," in *Climate Change 2013: The Physical Science Basis. Contribution of Working Group I to the Fifth Assessment Report of the Intergovernmental Panel on Climate Change* (Cambridge and New York: Cambridge University Press, 2013).

12. Elizabeth Chalecki, *He Who Would Rule: Climate Change in the Arctic and Its Implications for U.S. National Security,* Proceedings of the 48th Annual Convention of the International Studies Association (ISA) (Chicago, IL: ISA, 2007), 204–222.

13. United Nations Environment Program, *Climate in Peril: Projected Climate Change and Its Impacts,* available from grida.no, accessed 1/29/15.

14. Dale Jamieson, *A Companion to Environmental Philosophy* (Oxford: Blackwell, 2007), 1–531.

15. Max Oelschlaeger, *Caring for Creation: An Ecumenical Approach to the Environmental Crisis* (New Haven, CT: Yale University Press, 1994), 1–296.

16. William Johnson, "The Bible on Environmental Conservation: A 21st-Century Prescription," *Electronic Green Journal* 1, no. 12, art. 8 (Los Angeles: UCLA, 2000), 1–21.

17. Jim Ball, "The Use of Ecology in the Evangelical Protestant Response to the Ecological Crisis," *Perspectives on Science and Christian Faith,* 50:32–40, 1998; and Jim Ball, "Evangelicals, population and the ecological crisis," *Christian Scholars Review XXVIII:* 1994, 226–253.

18. Randy VanDragt, *"Species Stewardship: The Roles of Science, Ethics, and Faith* (Azusa, CA: Azusa Pacific University, 2008), 1–25.

19. Calvin DeWitt, "Ecology and Ethics: Relation of Religious Belief to Ecological Practice in the Biblical Tradition," *Biodiversity and Conservation*, 4:838–848, 1995.

Chapter 9

All of the following works contributed to my knowledge of this topic:

1. Hugh Ross, Kenneth Samples, and Mark Clark, *Lights in the Sky and Little Green Men: A Rational Christian Look at UFOs and Extraterrestrials* (Colorado Springs: NavPress, 2002); "Reasons to Believe," Covina, CA, available from reasons.org.

2. Michio Kaku, personal conversation. For more of his thoughts, see *Physics of the Impossible: A Scientific Exploration into the World of Phasers, Force Fields, Teleportation, and Time Travel* (New York: Doubleday, 2008).

3. Ross, Samples, and Clark, *Lights in the Sky,* 85.

4. Jacques Vallee, The Outpost Forum, available from theoutpostforum.com, accessed 1/28/15; UFO Researcher/ Astronomer/Computer Scientist, Euro-America Ventures.

5. Carmen DiCello, "UFO Theories: Some Proposals and Thought Provokers," available from angelfire.com/pa2/truthandthings/ufo.theories.html, accessed 1/28/15.

Conclusion

1. There is some dispute as to the original source of this quote. While commonly attributed to Saint Augustine, its origins are difficult to trace before 1617. It may have originated with Marco Antionio de Dominis in *De republica ecclesiastica libri X* 1, book 4, chapter 8 (London, 1617), 676.

About the Author

D R. LESLIE WICKMAN was born and raised in the Pacific Northwest. She graduated magna cum laude with a bachelor of arts in political science from Willamette University in Salem, Oregon. She later earned a master's degree in aero/astro engineering, as well as a doctoral degree in human factors and biomechanics, from Stanford University.

For over a decade she worked as an engineer for Lockheed Martin Missiles & Space in Sunnyvale, California. While there, she had the opportunity to work on NASA's Hubble Space Telescope and International Space Station Programs, and received commendations from both NASA and contractors for her contributions. During this time, she was designated as Lockheed's corporate astronaut.

Following Lockheed Martin, she moved to WET Labs in Universal City, California, where she was instrumental in the development and programming of the Fountains of Bellagio in Las Vegas, Nevada. After that she spent several years working as a research scientist with The RAND Corporation in Santa Monica, California, on technical and political aspects of various national defense issues.

She currently acts as chair of the engineering and computer science department, as well as director of the Center for Research in Science (CRIS), at Azusa Pacific University in Azusa, California. In addition, she serves as an engineering specialist on various aerospace projects. Currently, her primary research project involves investigating the effects of climate change on national security issues.

Leslie played women's professional football with the California Quake (Women's World Bowl Champions in 2002), as well as pro-am beach doubles volleyball with the FIVB and CBVA. She has traveled with Athletes in Action Volleyball to Bolivia, Brazil, and South Africa.

Dr. Wickman is also an ordained minister.

WORTHY®
PUBLISHING

IF YOU ENJOYED THIS BOOK, WILL YOU CONSIDER SHARING THE MESSAGE WITH OTHERS?

- Mention the book in a Facebook post, Twitter update, Pinterest pin, or blog post.

- Recommend this book to those in your small group, book club, workplace, and classes.

- Head over to facebook.com/worthypublishing, "Like" the page, and post a comment as to what you enjoyed the most.

- Tweet "I recommend reading #GodoftheBigBang by @LeslieWickman // @worthypub"

- Pick up a copy for someone you know who would be challenged and encouraged by this message.

- Write a book review online.

You can subscribe to Worthy Publishing's newsletter at worthypublishing.com.

WORTHY PUBLISHING
FACEBOOK PAGE

WORTHY PUBLISHING
WEBSITE